The
POWER
of Building Your
Bright Side

Five Surprising Renewal Strategies to
Personal and Business Success

Donna Rae Smith

Wynwood

A Division of Baker Book House Co
Grand Rapids, Michigan 49516

© 1995 by Donna Rae Smith

Published by Wynwood Press
a division of Baker Book House Company
P.O. Box 6287, Grand Rapids, MI 49516-6287

Previously published in 1991 by Wynwood Press as *Building Your Bright Side*

Second printing, October 1995

Printed in the United States of America

ISBN 0-922066-90-6

Unless otherwise noted, Scripture quotations are from the HOLY BIBLE, NEW INTERNATIONAL VERSION®. NIV®. Copyright © 1973, 1978, 1984 by International Bible Society. Used by permission of Zondervan Publishing House. All rights reserved.

Scripture quotations identified JB are from THE JERUSALEM BIBLE, copyright © 1966 by Darton, Longman and Todd, Ltd., and Doubleday and Company, Inc. Reprinted by permission of the publishers.

Scripture quotation identified KJV is from the King James Version of the Bible.

Grateful acknowledgment is made for permission to include the following:

Excerpts from *The Prophet*, by Kahlil Gibran. Copyright © 1923 by Khalil Gibran and renewed 1951 by Administrations C.T.A. of Kahlil Gibran and Mary G. Gibran. Reprinted by permission of Alfred A. Knopf, Inc.

"Jack Is Afraid of Jill," from *Knots* by R. D. Laing. Copyright © 1970 by R. D. Laing. Reprinted by permission of Pantheon Books, a division of Random House, Inc.

"Flowers Are Red," by Harry Chapin. Copyright © Story Songs Ltd., 1978.

"I have now read your book and it is delightful."

—W. Edwards Deming, Ph.D., consultant in statistical studies

"In this competitive world, any book that can encourage a spirit of individual entrepreneurism is bound to be a winner."

—Jack Trout, president, Trout & Partners, and author, *Positioning*

"Donna Rae has given us a true gift. By sharing deeply in her own experience as well as the lessons that she has learned from friendships and relationships, she has given us all a gift of inspiration and a pathway not only to success in business, but to success in life as well."

—Jack Kahl, chairman and CEO, Manco

"A book about inspiration. Not only inspiring your employees but also about inspiring yourself. A real jewel."

—F. Kenneth Iverson, chairman and CEO, Nucor Corporation

"Donna Rae Smith is gifted with a vision of life that can empower us all. Her new book is a masterwork of ideas and insights that illuminates our dark side in a way that is simple but yet profound. I recommend that you read this book because only then can you feel its power."

—George C. Fraser, president, Success Source, Inc., and author,
Success Runs in Our Race

"Donna Rae Smith packs the pages of *The Power of Building Your Bright Side* with laughter and inspiration, as well as solid information for business leaders. If you're preparing your organization for the demands of the 21st century, the first thing to do is read this book."

—L. M. Cook, chairman, ARCO

"*The Power of Building Your Bright Side* can be a guide for everyone who wants to come out of the darkness and become a bright candle—lighting your way and that of others."

—Bernie S. Siegel, M.D., author, *Love, Medicine, and Miracles*

"*The Power of Building Your Bright Side* really offers up a feast for our consumption, including appetizer and entree. I can hardly wait for coffee and dessert!"

—Frank E. Mosier, retired vice chairman, BP America

"What Donna Rae Smith understands so beautifully is something we all need to remember: business is—or ought to be—a form of personal expression. Her new book is a joyful reminder that the only route to endowing our efforts with meaning is to begin with self-knowledge. Towards that end, she serves as a warm and wise guide."

—Joshua Hyatt, senior editor, *Inc.* magazine

"Donna Rae Smith has ensured her place among the best management consultants by providing an inspirational, practical, easy-to-read success guide that will improve the readers, their employees, and their company. If you think one person can't make a difference in the world, you must read Donna Rae Smith's new book."

—Gregg A. Searle, executive vice president, Diebold Inc.

"Donna Rae's new book challenges and inspires the human spirit as only she can. Must reading for anyone who wants to unleash the power of involvement in their organization."

—Jim Krimmel, president, Zaclon, Inc. (Former Du Pont Division)

"Donna Rae Smith's prescription for improving your business by improving the quality of interpersonal relationships at your company rings true and crystal clear."

—Daniel J. Ramella, president and CEO, Penton Publishing

"Donna Rae Smith's book is an inspiration to business leaders. She provides unique insight into finding positive solutions in the workplace. Solving client problems is what we do every day and Donna Rae presents creative ways to find Bright Side answers that work."

—Kathleen C. Radebaugh, president, The Ohio Bank, Northeast Region

"Donna Rae Smith shatters ceilings, myths, and illusions obscuring authentic success and gives us five enduring guideposts to renaissance in turbulent times."

—Dr. Denis Waltley, author, *Empires of the Mind*

16821 Park Circle Drive
Chagrin Falls, Ohio 44023
440 – 543 – 1800
www: Bright-side.com

Contents

Acknowledgments

Bright Side is a daring adventure that frees the human spirit for the purpose of personal growth. My own adventure has only been possible through the learning and encouragement I have received from many dynamic individuals. There are a few people in particular whose unique qualities have each guided and inspired me throughout my journey. My publisher, Baker Book House Company, has provided endless encouragement and support.

My deepest gratitude to Bright Side's staff, Susan Weimer, Susan Powell, Jean Raymont, Kelley Anderson, and Patti Siko, whose contributions have enhanced and strengthened the value of Bright Side. The words of The Power of Building Your Bright Side have come to life under the expert editing guidance of John Ettorre, Mary Jane Skala, and Dan Van't Kerkhoff, Senior Editor at Baker Book House. I thank all of my friends, family, and associates who have contributed by believing in me. Finally, I applaud my precious family—my husband, Ed, my daughter, Maressa, and my son, Brant. My reverence to the women in my life whose hearts have nurtured the seed of my potential—special love to my grandmother, Domenica and my mother, Rosemary.

I would like to express my gratitude to the following businesses. I have learned as much from their leaders and heroes as they have learned from me.

Alcan Rolled Products Company • American Society of Women Accountants (ASWA) • American Steel & Wire Corporation • American Society of Interior Designers (ASID) • American Society of Association Executives (ASAE) • American Advertising Federation Convention • AT&T • Avery Specialty Tape (Division of Fasson) • Benjamin Moore & Company • British Petroleum of America • Catholic Youth Organization • Cleveland Advanced Manufacturing Program (CAMP) • Cohen & Company • Conferon, Inc. • Coopers & Lybrand • Council of Smaller Enterprises (COSE) • Cuyahoga County Public Library • Delphi Packard Electric Systems, GMC • Diabetes Association • Employers Resource Council • Forest City Commercial Management • Governor's Youth Board • Greater Cleveland Growth Association • Hackett & Arnold • Heart Warming Creations, Inc. • Hewlett-Packard • Hoffmann La Roche Inc. • Honda Manufacturing • Huntington National Bank • IBM • Inc. 500 Conference • InterBold/Diebold • The Internal Revenue Service • Johnstown America Corporation and Westfield Companies • The Junior League • Lubrizol • Manco, Inc. • NASA, Lewis Research Center • National City Bank • National Wellness Conference • Ohio Association of Personnel Consultants (OAPC) • The Ohio Manufacturers' Association • Original Cookie Company • Penton Publishing • The Power of Laughter & Play • Progressive Companies • Ronald McDonald House International Meeting/McDonald's Corp. • Rubbermaid, Inc. • Scott Fetzer & Co. • Siemens Energy & Automation, Inc. • Smythe Cramer Company • Star System, Inc. • Steel Service Center Institute • The Timken Company • United States District Court Northern District of Ohio Probation Office • Ursuline College • Women Life Underwriters Confederation (WLUC) • XEROX Corporation • Youth Opportunities Unlimited • Zaclon, Inc. (formerly DuPont)

Extraordinary people in working America inspire us to continue to learn from each other as well as ourselves.

> If you think you went far enough, go a little further.
> —John Westlake, The Timken Company

> Change and survival have the same meaning.
> —Dave Orr, The Timken Company

> Positive energy is contagious.
> —Judy Rodriguez, Heart Warming Creations, Inc.

> Don't retaliate, communicate.
> —Pete Hamryszak, Johnstown America

Introduction

Years ago, while hosting a morning television interview program in Norfolk, Virginia, I received a blessing, though I scarcely realized it at the time. I had the chance to interview a remarkable man, Dr. Norman Vincent Peale, the legendary author of *The Power of Positive Thinking*.

I remember being struck at the time by his humility and his softness, by the quiet manner in which he spoke. How could such a famous man, the author of nearly fifty books, be so unassuming? In my shallowness and spiritual poverty at that time, I couldn't understand it.

He told me in our interview that upon meeting a new person, he was in the habit of saying a brief prayer, asking God to let him like that person and that they would in turn like him. I didn't appreciate the power of that message at the time, but in the years since, that small seed he planted has taken root in the fertile soil of my own growing spiritual awareness. And as my life has unfolded, I've had the enormous good fortune to accumulate wisdom from other masters in various walks of life.

Besides my catalytic brush with Dr. Peale, who died at the age of ninety-five on Christmas Eve 1993, I've received inspirational boosts from the internationally respected quality expert Dr. W. Edwards Deming, Wal-Mart founder Sam Walton, and world-class marathon runner Allison Roe from New Zealand. I met Dr. Deming after I traveled to Japan, and I hosted Ms. Roe in my home. My familiarity with Walton came second-hand, through his business disciple Jack Kahl, who later became my client.

More important than any of these influences—in fact, the one that helped stitch them together into a coherent pattern—is my deepening relationship with Christ, whom I accepted as my Savior some years ago when my life hit bottom.

Today, after working several years in television and then in the machine tool industry, I coach organizations, including Fortune 500 companies, on how to put into motion the lessons I've learned about change management, valuing the individual, and injecting fun and spirit into our lives and thus our work. This is primarily a business book, but it is a business book based on working with the core of human beings—their spirit. Therefore, it can impact everything in your life.

The stakes for this country's businesses, schools, and other institutions in establishing a spiritual and competitive renewal are enormous. As we face today's highly competitive global marketplace, which places a premium on inventiveness and constant improvement, we're forced to tap every available source for creativity and enhanced productivity.

It is the intangible mental energies of individual people that will make a competitive difference for the organization and bring a real sense of purpose and meaning to the individuals as well. We can bring to our life's work our heart, our passion, our ability to think and risk and create. But to do so, we often must be prepared to reinvent our deeply cherished patterns of thinking and operating, which are so often counterproductive.

That message is beginning to register, even in the highest reaches of corporate America. In the 1993 annual report to its shareholders, the General Electric Company's chairman and CEO, Jack Welch, Jr., discusses how GE's "boundaryless behavior" in pursuit of becoming the world's low-cost producer of high-quality goods and services led to the best financial results in the company's century-plus history.

"We are betting everything on our people—empowering them, giving them the resources, and getting out of their way—and the numbers tell us that this focus has not only pointed us in the right direction but is providing us with a momentum that is accelerating," writes Welch, formerly known more for slashing jobs than introducing non-traditional management tactics. Welch says 1993 was "a year when our soft initiatives turned increasingly into hard results."

These "soft" means—building organizations around the people who run them and counting on ordinary workers to supply fresh ideas—are nothing short of revolutionary for American business. The old way of doing things for companies was hierarchical, based on the football model. Information and direction flowed from top to bottom. The new way is a level playing field, rather like a soccer team model.

Today, the successful leader is a coach, a person who inspires, encourages, and offers suggestions. Leaders are most valuable not when they are directing subordinates in the details of their jobs, but when they help them grow personally and professionally, thereby becoming greater assets to the larger organization.

Wal-Mart founder Sam Walton, as widely studied as any American leader in the second half of the twentieth century, liked to say that his most important task as a leader was to instill self-esteem in his people. Why is such a soft area so vital to the bottom line? Because employees will treat customers the way they themselves are treated.

But this renewal must begin with an end to buck-passing. To initiate profound personal, spiritual change, we must begin by focusing the searchlight of truth inward, to honestly take an accounting of ourselves in order to understand how we short-circuit our own success and consequently that of our team and our entire organization. We must realize the impediments to our success before we can begin removing them. This book seeks not only to heighten your awareness of the problems that might block you from your potential, but also to lay out a series of action steps you can implement in various areas of your life.

I'll discuss how some visionaries have built environments that foster risk-taking, encourage self-trust, and allow people to take potentially productive leaps of faith. This book is filled with insights on how good leaders I've worked with and observed shift paradigms and remove barriers to success, both for themselves and their organizations. It describes how they boldly venture into the often uncharted waters of unorthodoxy to create nurturing learning environments that are truly open to fundamental rethinking of tasks, spontaneous behavior, and a brisk spirit of experimentation.

We'll explore how to encourage individual entrepreneurship within the larger group and how to create organizations that both explicitly and implicitly state that everyone's input is welcomed and vital. And, perhaps most importantly, we'll find out how to have fun implementing these ideas. As one enlightened manager, Peter Wilzbach, puts it, effective people and effective groups "can't be all doom and gloom." Perhaps to be more successful in life and in work, we need to loosen our collars a bit and be less like we think we're supposed to be and more like we actually are.

I've found that the more troubled a person or an organization is, the more defensive the behavior will be. In fact, until recently, the primary coping strategy of Americans seemed to be denial, a dogged refusal to face up to the truth. I hope this book will inspire you to consider other, healthier patterns. The whole point of being inventive and innovative in the marketplace, after all, is to produce something that people value. If an organization hopes to produce something the world values, it must bring to the job elements that are truly unique to it—in other words, its people. So our discussion begins, and steadfastly remains, centered around individual spiritual rebirth.

In my own life, which for years was marked by deep divisions between heart (courage and passion) and spirit (energy and vitality) as well as by counterproductive thinking patterns, I have found that we really do have a choice: We choose our own thoughts, our own mental models of what is possible. And then we act upon them. We can choose to be trapped. We can believe the negative, hurtful things that others—sometimes even those we love—have said to and about us. Or we can choose to be free. We can erect our own scaffolding of truth by turning elsewhere for support and loving encouragement and believing what God says is true about us.

It is through the process of choosing healthy living patterns over unhealthy ones that God can reach us with opportunities. Then it is only through our own choices that we can grasp ahold of these opportunities. When we think we are unable to change, we destroy our peace of mind, dignity, and self-respect. God has a real purpose for each and every tender life. It is when we are able to step out of the darkness of destructive habits and into the light of God's Word that we begin to achieve clarity about our reason for being.

There is great harvest from the truth, I've learned time and again. I hope you'll begin today to sow it in your own life.

Part 1

Discover the Bright Side Inside Yourself

At Bright Side, we work with the inner core of people. Simply put, we labor to unblock those habits or traits that prevent learning and readiness to change and emphasize habits or traits that enhance change.

The Bright Side approach tutors people on breaking through that hard outer shell that so many unconsciously erect to protect themselves from hurt. We encourage people to let go of fear, discouragement, and other barriers and replace these toxic emotions with the fresh air of trust, truth, and belief.

Through interactive learning experiences, we can all learn to become risk-takers. We can grasp how to begin applying what we've learned in instituting real change in our lives. As the accompanying diagram suggests, positive change begins with focusing on our inner core. To prepare ourselves for meaningful growth and change, we must first buttress our self-esteem, self-respect, and self-trust.

So often our reaction to failure in life is similar to the experience of being trapped in a pair of Chinese handcuffs. They are a novelty item that can trap two fingers in a grip. If you've ever tried to get them off, you quickly learn that by simply acting on long-reinforced habit, which suggests pulling your fingers in opposite directions, their grip will only be tightened. Trying harder only makes matters worse, further tightening the pressure. Isn't that how we generally react when things aren't working on the job or in our personal lives? Don't we often merely try more of the same? Perhaps what we need is an entirely different approach.

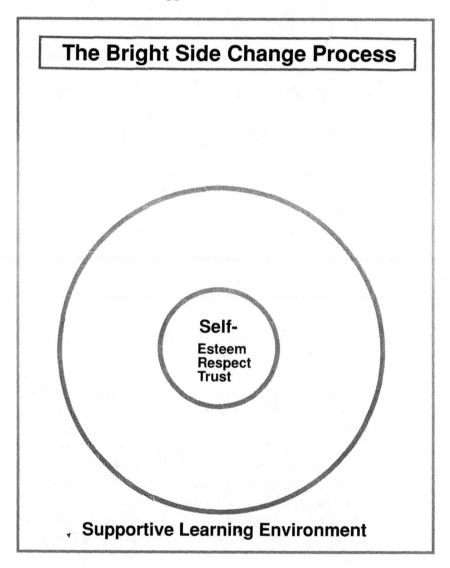

1

Shattering Illusions

In the late '70s, I was physically, emotionally, and spiritually at the lowest level I had ever been. I was alone, and at that point in my life, I dreaded solitude. I feared what I might find inside. As a child from a dysfunctional family and as an adult with some addictions, I feared that all of the accusations and criticisms I had heard and played back in my own mind might very well be true.

For years I had considered myself a positive person. And yet, somehow, it all changed. Somehow it was all wrong. How could a positive person be so filled with the rage that I felt? I was consumed with anger and self-doubt.

Along with many other baby boomers, I had chosen to follow what I thought to be the American way, only to discover that my American dream was filled with bad thinking, mediocrity, false beliefs, addictive behavior, complacency, greed, apathy, and diseased attitudes. In other words, I was following a path of darkness.

My problems were compounded by the greatest controlling force in the universe—fear. In this case it was a fear generated by childhood experiences and reinforced by rigid formal education. I suffered from a fear of appearing foolish, of being rejected, of failure. I feared the unknown and I feared change. Consequently, I feared the possibility of growth and of taking personal responsibility for my life.

My first glimpse of the truth came in the early '80s. Until then, I pretended to have a perfect family, a perfect marriage, and a perfect career, when in fact I was from a family that hid alcoholism, a marriage that perpetuated destructive habits, and a business dominated by intimidation and adversarial relationships.

I began to see the American dream was not working for me or for many others. That realization was crystallized in 1981 by a chain of events that included the breakup of my marriage and the loss of my job. It was through pain and the end of denial and blaming others that my life was transformed. But it wasn't by choice; the events were thrust upon me.

I started in the machine tool industry as a sales executive for a family-owned business and later became a manager and officer in the company. In 1981, Ohio was the machine tool capital of the world, but I had the misfortune of working in the business when it became the first major industry in the state to be hit hard by competition from Japanese manufacturers.

The American machine tool giants had been manufacturing the same machines year after year. Prices increased, delivery times lengthened, and yet features remained the same. Even the lackluster appearance of the equipment didn't change; the machines were always painted the same drab machine-tool gray or green. But that didn't matter, we thought, because in the perception of American manufacturers our products were superior. Though our country is known for fostering individuality, it was, paradoxically, producing industries that were comfortable with uniformity, locking out learning, change, flexibility, and innovation.

I fit into the larger cycle of the business by not rocking the boat, by not generating new ideas, by not really hearing the needs of my customers, by not thinking, by not caring for my business associates. This approach was successful until I experienced the devastation triggered by Japan's creative approach to machine tools.

I heard that the Japanese were stealing everything from America, from ideas to technology. But by traveling to Japan in 1981 to tour the manufacturing facilities of three companies—Nakamura-Tome,

Okuma-Howa, and Toshiba—I discovered that Japanese theft was an American myth. What I found instead were Japanese attitudes of caring customer service that contrasted sharply with our own then-sterile concepts of service and a willingness to foster creativity and innovation that extended to offering whatever customers wanted in designs, features, and colors. I also learned that the Japanese encouraged their workers to be flexible, creative, open, and optimistic. They accomplished this through exercises, songs, cheers, even prayer and meditation. Finally, and perhaps most importantly, I noted that the Japanese treated children as treasures.

What I saw in Japan caused me deep concern. I began to think that the devastation of the American machine tool industry was a precursor to similar troubling patterns in other sectors of American manufacturing. I thought it was unfair. I had entered the business with one purpose in mind: to make money. And so when the industry began to crumble, I crumbled along with it. I had no soul. I had no spirit. I had no purpose. I had spent my most precious gift—time—following false beliefs. When everything collapsed, I discovered that I was living a lie. I didn't know who I was. I realized that money could never replace an inner sense of purpose and happiness. My anger turned into illness.

Finally, it was illness—a facial skin disorder—that shattered me. I could not look at myself in the mirror. Whenever I did I was reminded of my deep inner pain and conflict. To me, my face had become the outward manifestation of what was wrong with my life. Only later did I realize that God had brought me to my knees physically to make me understand the profound importance of the mind and spirit.

I was filled with rage, a rage wrapped in a shield of self-denial and fear that kept me from making changes. I had learned this fear from my family. It was reinforced by schools and by our corporate culture. Control by fear keeps everyone in line but locks out new ideas, creativity, imagination, innovation, enthusiasm, health, spirit, and God. Indeed, it locks out who I am.

In the machine tool industry, I had learned lessons of ruthless competition: to lead by intimidation and fear and never take total responsibility for actions (it is much easier to blame or to attack).

In this mode, denial is so great that the true self is buried under the guise of looking good. Not once did it cross my mind that there were other methods of leadership or that I could personally bring about change.

Whenever I did suggest change, my ideas were rejected. Creative ideas were scoffed at because they came from people who knew little about financial statements. But the financial statements were showing that money was being lost. The only solutions being offered, and followed, were those of cutting back on expenses and staff or selling more. My suggestion of providing a more comprehensive warranty service for the machines was met with "It's too costly" and "We've never done it that way." The concept of trying another way was yet to be discovered. Meanwhile, the Japanese listened to the needs of America.

From devastation in the machine tool industry, in marriage, in physical health and appearance, I reached my personal low. I worked for money; the money was gone. I married for security; the security was gone. I lived for appearances; the appearances were gone. I was living in a deep, dark hole. It was the journey of finding a way out that inspired Bright Side concepts.

It is not easy to break through years of barriers, fear, and erroneous beliefs. But I discovered one key: The past held creative energy, particularly from early childhood, before my family and educators locked me into single-mode thinking.

In my pain, or because of my pain, I knew change would occur. I was going to take action. But how could I change and take action when all that I knew was the following and gathering of information?

One evening, alone in my bedroom, I began to consider my life. Everything was still and quiet. Quite by accident, with nowhere else to turn, I began to review my life as though it were a movie, frame by frame, life experience by life experience. Initially frightened by what I might uncover, I experienced the moods and emotions of each memory and made a decision as to what I would do with those feelings.

I experienced the negative feelings and then let them go either by burning out the frame or by diminishing and thereby completely reducing the hurtful image and its impact. *How simple,* I thought to myself. The positive past experiences, which were hard to find, were made powerful by enlarging them. These positive experiences were visually enhanced by increasing the size, the intensity, and the brilliance of color. By evening's end, I had a movie of my bright side! I felt totally engulfed in love, goodness, hope, joy, and optimism.

That was the first key to unlocking the prison that held captive the creative spirit God has given to me, the resourceful brilliance that exists within all of us. Without really knowing it at the time, I had the experience of being filled with God, a power much greater than the human power, a power that released my inner spirit. When I discovered that I was an empty shell, filled with darkness, I discovered God. It was in darkness that I experienced the divine. I realize today that those dark memories cut me off from God. But we all have the ability to choose a different path.

2

That Quiet Inner Voice

Some time ago, my son was in the hospital and was diagnosed with diabetes. The weekend he was released was a joyful one for our family. So on Sunday morning, we decided to walk several blocks into our village for breakfast. Returning home, we were met with a light spring rain. My daughter and son were delighted by the soft raindrops. They played under the light coat I held out for them. And I, in turn, delighted in their laughter, grateful that Brant was once again home, doing better under the control of insulin.

But a few moments later we were deluged without warning by a fierce rainstorm. Soaked by the downpour, I was miserable. Now I was lamenting our predicament and feeling waves of irritation well up inside. My children, however, were in ecstasy, laughing and skipping. Their glee irritated me more as I began to consider the details of changing clothes in order to prepare for church, wondering if we would be on time, and the nuisance of it all.

Then I heard my children laugh louder and begin to sing "Singing in the Rain." Perhaps it was the laughter, or the familiarity of the catchy Gene Kelly tune, or perhaps it was the rain that cleared my brain, but I realized at that moment that I could not do a thing about the circumstances. I could, however, do something about my response to them. So I decided to join my children.

The three of us laughed, skipped, danced, and sang—in the rain! It was a freeing, joyful moment, leaving me feeling totally cleansed of any irritation. My neighbor later told me that when he saw us skipping home he wished he had captured our happiness with his video camera.

That night, I dreamed about storms. In my dream, there was blackness. Then, in the middle of this darkness, there appeared a beautiful, ruffled, rainbow-colored umbrella. I wished for an umbrella just like that.

That week, while making a presentation at a hospital, I passed the gift shop. For the first time in my life I heard the quiet inner voice that people often remark about. I was directed to enter the shop to find the rainbow-colored umbrella from my dream. How irrational this was! First, to hear an inner voice and then to even consider going into a gift shop to find the umbrella of my dreams.

There I stood outside the gift shop, contemplating what to do. After all, I pondered, a bright, educated woman even thinking about looking for something from her dream was pretty crazy!

After some struggle, I mustered the courage to go in. I asked the shopkeeper for an umbrella and her eyes lit up. She said that she had only one umbrella left and that she would get it for me. She brought out an umbrella that was identical to the one in my dream— a fully ruffled rainbow-colored umbrella.

I found it only by listening to that quiet inner voice, my intuition. Yet, how often we do not trust and listen to our inner voice because it is not logical or proper. Think of the countless solutions we have overlooked because we didn't trust our own inner sense. We have all had the experience of thinking, *I wish I'd said that*. Often, the unspoken idea is the key to the puzzle.

Psychologist Carl R. Rogers says:

> One of the basic things which I was a long time in realizing, and which I am still learning, is that when an activity feels as though it is valuable or worth doing, it is worth doing. Put another way, I have learned that my total . . . sensing of a situation is more trustworthy than my intellect.

All of my professional life I have been going in directions which others thought were foolish, and about which I have had doubts myself. But I have never regretted moving in directions which "feel right" even though I have oftentimes felt lonely or foolish.

I have found that when I have trusted some inner nonintellectual sensing, I have discovered wisdom in the move. In fact, I have found that when I have followed one of these unconventional paths because it felt right or true, then in five or ten years many of my colleagues have joined me, and I no longer need to feel alone in it.[1]

We generally feel awkward putting credence in intuition. The critical self constantly repeats those negative statements we have learned that teach us not to feel or rely on our intuition. "Don't cry," or "Don't whine," we were often told. "Don't speak that way" and "Don't be selfish." "Don't pay attention to that," and above all, "Don't be so sensitive."

I have heard hundreds of stories from people about meeting spouses, avoiding tragedy, and being at the right place at the right time as a direct result of paying attention to the quiet inner voice. Indeed, as we seek our successes in business, science, or the arts, we often find those achievements were first imagined as mental pictures springing from our own rich inner treasure.

Creative geniuses such as Mozart, Kipling, Goethe, and Brahms spoke of their discoveries as being inspired by intuition, mental images, or a divine source. It's not hard to conclude that many of our treasured experiences or valued inventions come from trusting our thoughts, ideas, and mental images.

We can access this power not only occasionally, but also daily. However, when we are filled with apprehension, tension, or mistrust, it is often difficult to be aware of our internal voices. In a world filled with the distractions of the media and work it is often difficult to listen. We are not only failing to plant healthy thinking seeds, but we are also failing to tend to the fruit that wants to ripen within. The fruits we bear are great ideas or the special gifts—like the rainbow umbrella—that we can receive in only one way: by listening to and trusting the quiet inner sense.

3

The Power of Emotions

An exceptionally successful, caring, and wealthy man was institutionalized, overwhelmed by the rage of his repressed anger. When he was a young man, he and his father had argued. When the man was thirty, his father, sixty, had abandoned the family. He never came back. Some thirty years later, at the very same age, on the exact date, the son broke down, unable to function as those intense feelings began to erupt and emerge. He remained numb to his feelings until they could no longer be contained. Perhaps he is a product of our culture, where the wounded inner child continues to contaminate our adult lives.

The author John Bradshaw maintains that all of us, to some extent, come from dysfunctional families, and that we carry within us a wounded inner child. This child is responsible for our violence and cruelty. It is the cause of our addictions—whether to substances, people, or activities. We often numb ourselves to feeling and pain by addiction. It is estimated that there are 131 million addicts in our society. The wounded inner child will dog us and interfere with our lives until we stop evading our pain.

My life is proof of the doggedness of the wounded inner child. At seven, I insisted my father didn't love me. My mother followed the rules of appearance-management she had been taught, and she corrected what I knew inside to be true, what I thought, felt, and saw. "Your father loves you. He doesn't call, write, or visit because I asked him not to. He certainly loves you," she said. What a destructive and confusing message! I learned not to believe or trust what I thought, felt, or saw. I equated love with absence, abandonment, and abuse. The image I grasped was that of being hugged and stabbed at the same time.

I was not allowed to verbally express my anger, yet it kept surfacing. Enraged as a child, I took scissors to my wooden toy chest and gouged its surface. "Sweet girls don't do that," I was told. Enraged as an adult, I turned the volcanic anger inward, causing colitis and then a skin disorder. I rejected myself and then married a man who also sometimes rejected me. I knew something was amiss. My continually acting out my anger interfered with my life until I began healing the wounded inner child that denies feelings as a strategy to cope with pain.

My life had all the symptoms John Bradshaw lists of the wounded child. As we view wounded child questionnaires and wounded child indexes of suspicion, we see that issues of fear and mistrust dominate as indicators of a wounded child within. Some of Bradshaw's indicators of a wounded child:

- Mistrust of people
- Fear of abandonment
- Fear of trying new experiences
- Fear of anger
- Fear of saying "no" directly
- Trouble identifying what you are feeling
- Difficulty in expressing your feelings
- Excessive competitiveness
- Intense fear of making a mistake

Is this the same fear, lack of trust, and emotional numbness that is operating in today's corporate environment? At one company, when Bright Side workshop participants talked about experiences of being loved, one man said all of his memories were of violence and cruelty, of being physically and verbally abused. According to Bradshaw, when we are not loved for the precious, tender prize we are, we develop a deep spiritual wound. We need unconditional love.

In Bright Side sessions, I have discovered that some people struggle to recall a positive childhood experience. Some people are so deeply wounded that it is hard to celebrate joyful childhood memories because so much feeling is toxic and so much is repressed.

Yet, inside each of us, there is this delightful kid filled with wonder, resiliency, joy, courage, and adventure—our own unique being. This joyful child can only be released when we are able to free the wounded child by expressing our feelings.

My healing started when a situation with my mother triggered the rage, pain, and abandonment of my childhood. In therapy, my inner child then confronted that anger and lack of protection. In a subsequent session, my mother herself nurtured and loved that hurting, inner Donna Rae. How blessed and fortunate I was to have my mother be courageous enough to attend the session! It allowed the child frozen within by fear, hurt, and anger to be free of this contamination.

I was once given an article about ceramic cups that people used to cry into—cups to save your tears. The Hebrews kept two kinds of tear cups—one for when they were sad and one for when they were happy. The fullness of the cups reflected their owner's spirit. The more tears in the cup, the fuller the cup, the more that person was esteemed. Imagine, high esteem for people who are fully alive with emotion, people who care and are filled with passion and compassion, people who easily cry for joy, people who cry for pain! An added benefit is that according to scientific research, crying is cleansing, ridding us of the toxic biochemicals produced by stress.

We need to feel the full range of emotion in our lives and in our work. We need to care about the violence in our world. We need to become fully alive to the pain and joy of our world. We must laugh and cry to show we are persons who care deeply, who are sensitive to ourselves and to others.

In many therapeutic programs, individuals hold dolls or stuffed animals to help access and thaw their deep feelings. Even though as children we are naturally trusting, we have learned not to trust ourselves. We have been taught that the things we feel, think, see, and say aren't actually what we feel, think, see, or say. And our school and workplace environments often continue to reinforce that harmful learning by stifling fearlessness and creativity. We have been robbed of our sense of wonder, joy, love, play, feeling, and emotion. No wonder the corporate climate views these qualities as inappropriate! The dysfunction has been carried into the working world. How can the spirit of individuals and the spirit of a team of employees be reawakened without feeling, without love, and without fun?

Can you picture your own precious inner child, the beautiful child you once were? Can you nurture, accept, and love that being of wonder? Can we as managers and leaders facilitate the nurturing of self and of others? Can we show people that we love them as they are? Can we help re-parent one another by reflecting each other's goodness and worthiness? Can we accept and cherish each other's differences so that in our work we can fully celebrate and utilize individual uniqueness?

Each May, Revco, Inc., a drug-store chain, hosts a marathon and ten-kilometer race in Cleveland. Thousands of people compete. While running the Revco 10K one year, I was awed by wheelchair participants. As each one passed, my heart swelled with excitement and tenderness. Many of us cheered and applauded their courage. Overwhelmed by the intensity of my feeling, I realized that we were each cheering and applauding our own disabled inner being waiting to be freed.

Experiences I have had with organizations clearly show that teams can surpass individual performance. Can you imagine how much more powerful and effective teams would be if people were free to be exactly who they are? The energy used to repress self and emotion would then be available for much greater individual and team purposes. We would no longer be focused on what's wrong with ourselves, but on a sense of doing our unique creative work.

Feelings are energy. Denying feelings can distort our behavior and judgment, obscuring our perceptions, and crippling us and our relationships.

Without feelings, we lack authenticity and spontaneity, thus blocking our ability to know and be sensitive to ourselves and others.

When our emotions are blocked, our needs are not met and our positive energy turns into distress or dysfunctional behavior. We become defensive and rejecting. We judge, criticize, withdraw, and become hostile. We erect a protective shield of cold logic, keeping us emotionally distant and cut off from our creative right hemisphere of the brain. Logic causes us to focus on facts and avoid feelings.

Author David Johnson once wrote, "A person without feelings is not a person at all; he or she is a machine. What we need more of has been suppressed, denied, deadened . . . the heart and spirit of people."[2]

4

Transforming

In our culture, we have learned that work is serious and that peak performance comes from intensity. But think of athletes preparing for peak performance. It's common to see them in loose, relaxed, and playful behavior to reduce pre-performance stress. Or think of your own performance. You may have noticed that it is enhanced when you are relaxed and joyful, not when you are serious and intense.

It's easy to feel tension strangling our ability to think clearly and creatively. One philosopher wrote that playfulness may be the only ingredient necessary for creativity. Albert Einstein wrote about having free play with concepts. It is the child within that helps us unlock our rich inner treasure of individual talent and thinking.

Transforming by Validation

Good leaders recognize the importance of building self-esteem in others. How do they do that? They begin by validating others, by encouraging and believing in them.

I introduced the Starpower concept at the *Inc.* 500 Conference. Starpower is based on the principle that each of us has an underlying need to be validated, appreciated, valued, and loved. After being asked about the last time they received a gold star, Bright Side participants are encouraged to give and receive positive feedback and to keep record of their energy level and mood states during the process.

Participants are sometimes uncomfortable with being positive about themselves and with giving and receiving positive feedback. This is not surprising, for many of us have had more experience with negative or critical feedback. In fact, Jesuit psychologist John Powell documents in his book, *Happiness Is an Inside Job,* that many of us up until the age of five have received an average of more than four hundred daily comments that are limiting, negative, or critical. These comments, along with many other "ought-to" statements, have shaped and conditioned us.

But we can change the effect these influences have had on us. We can, in fact, erase the negative and begin fresh and new each day by replacing negative thoughts with joyful, awesome, loving, affirming thoughts.

- *I am unworthy* to *I am worthy.*
- *I am unlovable* to *I am lovable.*
- *I am of little value* to *I am valuable.*
- *I am insignificant* to *I am awesome.*
- *I am guilty* to *I am free of guilt.*
- *I bear grudges* to *I forgive myself and others.*
- *I fill with the negative* to *I let go of the negative and fill with the positive.*
- *I live on the dark side* to *I live on the bright side.*

Living on the bright side means to transform negative thinking to positive thinking, to hear and receive within our heart the positive feedback that we so often reject. We reject compliments because of the barriers of darkness we have built up as children. It is the giant Goliath, this garbage thinking that we have made so powerful. This negative thinking can make us slaves to addictions that are harmful to our well-being.

Each week I attend the international Bible Study Fellowship. It's a renewing experience, and it often reminds me of how, to a great extent, many of our values and principles are based on the Bible. At one of our Bible study sessions, Janeen, the leader, spoke of her own inability to accept positive feedback. She shared how one of her friends suggested opening the top of her shirt to let in a positive remark and to allow it to nurture her by gently patting it as it entered through this opening.

As we left this session, Janeen spoke to me and then playfully pulled open the top of my shirt to let in the compliment she had just given me, one that I had not even heard! I had not heard her words of encouragement because my armor of negativity was so strong that morning. There are times when we not only consciously reject or question goodness, but also when we can't even feel goodness to let it in because of the numbness we have developed to protect ourselves from pain.

Receiving compliments is like receiving love—it takes practice. Today, record each compliment you receive by opening the top of your shirt to ensure that you receive it fully and completely into your heart. While it is actually a good thing to receive compliments fully, our society has conditioned us to think that it is immature to place too much importance on them. Begin each day triumphantly and victoriously, working on renewing the mind by stretching out of the comfort zone of doubt, fear, and negative feedback and entering a new, joyful world open to encouragement, coaching, and positive feedback.

Transforming by Fun

Let me give you an example of transforming a negative situation by a spirit of fun. When I was asked to speak at the *Inc.* 500 Conference honoring America's fastest-growing, privately held corporations, I felt a mixture of blood-rushing excitement and nerve-racking fear. Certainly, if there was an audience that was highly motivated, this would be the one. It could also be my most sophisticated and challenging audience.

The morning that I was to travel to Raleigh, North Carolina, there were heavy thunderstorms in Cleveland—not the kind of weather in which I enjoy traveling. As I prepared to leave for my office, I received a shocking phone call from the dry cleaner. They could not locate the suit I was to wear for my presentation! I became frustrated and had to remind myself that I was supposed to be the expert on positive motivation and releasing stress. I was promised that they would try to find my one-of-a-kind suit.

One hour prior to leaving for Raleigh, the dry cleaner telephoned once again. They found my suit, but it was still dirty. They promised, however, to get it cleaned in one hour. Frazzled, I drove through heavy traffic to get my precious presentation suit. Deep relaxation breathing couldn't begin to wash away the mounting tension and the anxiety that was enveloping me.

Arriving at the airport with not a moment to spare, I decided to park in the garage for quicker access to the airport terminal. But I became more anxious when I could not find a parking space. After what seemed an endless search, I finally found a space and raced off to the terminal.

For the first time in my life, airport security stopped me. They wanted to inspect my briefcase. Rough hands pulled out all of the contents, only to discover that the suspicious item was a crucifix my sister had given to me. Eventually, deemed harmless, I was cleared, and I rapidly made my way to the gate at the far end of the terminal.

Once there, however, I was struck by the absence of other passengers. The plane had been delayed, I was told. I took in a breath of relief. At least I had enough time to go to the bathroom.

I hurried in the direction of the restroom signs, pushed open the door and found a stall. I was thinking about the trip and my speech, and I sighed with relief that I had not missed my flight. Then I walked out of the stall. I gasped. There, before my very eyes, was a man with his back to me—using the urinal. I was overwhelmed and hurried back into the stall, pulling the door behind me. I didn't know what to do. I couldn't stay in the bathroom all day. My anxiety level soared. Every muscle in my body tensed with fear and embarrassment. I didn't want this man or any other man to see me in the men's bathroom.

I slouched back in the corner of the stall sulking and feeling sorry for myself. Then I heard a zipping sound. The sound of a man zipping up his pants triggered the five-year-old that lives within me, and I got the giggles. I kept the giggling down deep inside. It felt good, like bubbles of happiness bursting in my body. All of my worries and anxiety were swept away. That internal laughter caused all of my tension to vanish.

I was holding back outrageous laughter as this man took forever to wash his hands, comb his hair, and unzip his pants to tuck in his shirt (of course)! That was all I needed. The silent giggles became an uproar. I burst out of the stall, profusely apologizing. "Oh, I am so sorry," I managed to apologize amidst the fits of laughter. By stark contrast, he didn't see anything funny. The look on his face told me he didn't believe me.

I knew I had to get out of there before I encountered another man. Immediately, I spun myself around and there, standing right in front of me, was one of the most handsome men I had ever seen, laughing at me! *What a relief,* I thought. At least this one is laughing.

He proceeded to talk to me, right there in the men's bathroom. He told me that he had been in the stall next to me and had heard me when I first came in. He thought he was the one who had made the mistake! We roared together. As we were preparing to leave the men's room laughing together, in walked another woman entering the men's bathroom!

Laughter, called "internal jogging" by the author Norman Cousins, is a simple and playful way to break tension and to release that highly optimistic, enthusiastic, wonderful kid that lives inside all of us. Laughter and humor may be our greatest coping mechanisms, and when used in the men's bathroom they can also be a useful way to meet good-looking men!

At an IBM meeting, one executive asked his people to come up with a laughter quota. And at a national meeting of a major real estate development company, attendees were asked to laugh for no reason at all. The next day many of them confided that they laughed just to laugh while they were driving, and even that made a difference in their attitude and how they felt.

At Loma Linda University, Dr. Lee Berk has researched the effect of laughter and humor on the human body. Dr. Berk found that laughter and humor reduce the toxic biochemicals produced by stress.

I recall watching my favorite sport at the Winter Olympics—ice skating. The Canadian competitor, Elizabeth Manley—who publicly stated that she went through therapy to help her learn to skate simply for the pure joy of the experience—received the silver medal. American competitor Debi Thomas, on the other hand, who was overly intense and serious, repeatedly stumbled, costing her the predicted gold medal and landing her the bronze.

We can't ask people to have fun only occasionally. That would be like asking people for occasional excellence. We must be in the habit of fun in order for it to work to our advantage.

Part 2

Recover Bright Side Moments of Childhood

In order to break through our natural fear of change and replace it with an eagerness for new ideas and learning, we must confront what is so often the source of both our pain and our mental barriers: our past. For far too many of us the past is full of negative lessons, bad memories from childhood that have helped establish grooves of inertia from which we've never extricated ourselves.

But even the worst childhood also contained glimpses of encouragement, models of hopeful possibilities. These should be the building blocks upon which we shape our healthier mental models of what is possible in our later lives. It's only through deeper self-awareness that we can learn to make better choices. As the diagram suggests, we can learn to release attitudes that cause us to resist change and self-improvement, and build on those that support learning environments.

We can begin by reviewing some key turning points in our early lives and trying to understand the choices to which they have led—both helpful and harmful. We can begin by recovering happy moments. By mentally reliving those experiences and fortifying ourselves with their liberating mental and emotional effects, we can begin to repair the hurt of the years.

From that beginning, we can redirect our lives down paths filled with adventure and a zest for the new and untried experience. We can take personal charge of transforming our future.

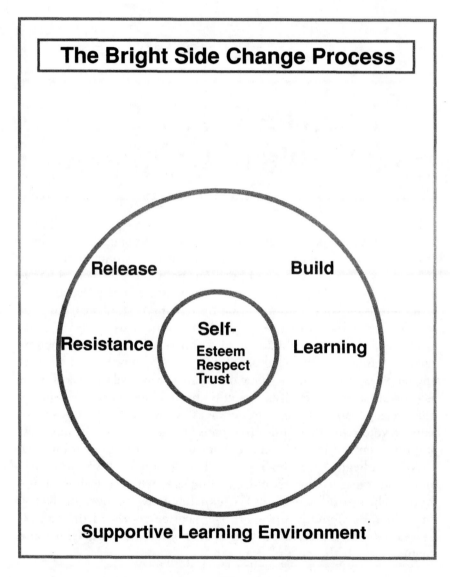

5

Finding Your Red Ball Jets

Another big breakthrough in changing my life came through meeting Allison Roe. Allison, a native of New Zealand, set the 1981 women's record for the twelfth New York City Marathon. About that time, business and training obligations brought her to Cleveland, and I had the unusual opportunity to have her as a guest in my house during her stay. A friend had brought us together, thinking that knowing Allison would be good for me.

I felt a real surge of excitement, the first excitement I had felt in a very long time. Never before had I had the privilege of being that close to a world-class champion. I was immediately impressed by Allison. She was warm and friendly and genuinely interested in sharing her knowledge and experiences with me. I instinctively knew she was a champion role model of excellence. We best learn from role models.

The contrast between the two of us was stark. She bubbled confidence, zest, joy, and hope. I was depressed. I felt almost lifeless when she entered my life, but she gave me invaluable training tools that helped transform me, erasing my dark way of thinking. Her presence in my life became the spark that ignited my current life's work.

I had invited my friends who were runners and athletes to meet Allison. Much to my surprise, what we learned from her went far beyond sports. As she began to talk about marathon training, I knew the time had arrived for me to accelerate my learning curve.

Believing You Can Win

When Allison described how she trained for a marathon, she focused almost exclusively on mental preparation. I began to cling to her every word. She said that 90 percent of winning in anything was in the mind, caused by a positive mental attitude—in other words, believing you can win. Allison's approach to mental training begins with being positive. Secondly, she mentally pictures the event. In that scene, she sees herself in detail, including the race course and her competitors, down to the clothing they will be wearing. Finally, she tries to accompany that positive mental picture with an equally upbeat mood state.

At first, I could feel myself rejecting what she said. If she is a winner because she is positive, then that means I am depressed because of my negative thinking. Yet, I had every reason to be negative and depressed. Look at what the Japanese had done to us! (It certainly was not *my* fault, and it certainly had nothing to do with *my* thinking.) But as she continued describing these steps, a memory that I had completely repressed came roaring from my mind. It was a memory of an experience I had had as a five-year-old child living in Disco, Michigan.

The big event in Disco was the fair. Like most fairs, ours had amusement rides, pie-baking contests, cake-decorating contests, watermelon-eating contests, and races. I was interested in the race for boys and girls in grade school, so I went to my mother and told her I wanted to enter. She and I went to the big city of Utica to get a pair of Red Ball Jets. I believed that anybody who had those magic shoes could run faster and jump higher than anybody else. The minute we got those running shoes, I put them on and I began to practice for this race. Wearing my Red Ball Jets, I went out to a dusty country road with my mother and my Uncle Bob. They rode bicycles as I ran.

Every day we would practice. My mother would encourage me, saying things like, "Donna, you are fast!" And I remember thinking, *Of course I'm fast, I've got Red Ball Jets!* Then she would say, "Donna, you are a strong runner!" I would look down at my feet and say, *Yes, of course I'm a strong runner, I've got Red Ball Jets!* And my mother would say, "Donna, you are going to win that race!" And I'd look at those Red Ball Jets and think to myself, *Yes, of course I can, I've got Red Ball Jets!* We practiced for that race every day. I was using mental picturing without even knowing it.

The day of the race came. All seventy-five young participants took their places at the starting line. I looked down at my feet and saw those Red Ball Jets. I looked at the children to my right and to my left. I was the only one with Red Ball Jets! It was at that moment that I said to myself, *I'm the winner!* I knew in my heart and in my mind that I was going to win that race. That was my only thought.

I looked straight ahead at the starting line, focused on winning, focused on being the first person to reach the finish line. The starting person said, "On your mark, get set, go!" Off we went! Each of us ran as fast as we could, but there was only one person who took first place that day—me.

I had completely forgotten that winning experience because it had been buried under negative, critical thinking, the garbage thinking of my adulthood. As I recall that experience of victory when I was a five-year-old, I now realize that it would have been just as powerful had I taken second or third place. The experience taught me valuable lessons. Above all, it taught me to believe my dream.

Yes, there were children who were stronger and taller and faster. But the biggest difference between those other children and me that day was that I believed. I believed not in reality, but in potential. I believed that I could win the race. That was the only thought that went through my mind—winning. And, of course, I believed in the magic of Red Ball Jets.

As Scripture notes, we're called to clear up our minds. "Finally, brothers, whatever is true, whatever is noble, whatever is right, whatever is pure, whatever is lovely, whatever is admirable—if anything is excellent or praiseworthy—think about such things" (Phil. 4:8).

By mentally picturing joyful or otherwise desired outcomes, we can influence our behavior, even if we're merely fantasizing, because each of our thoughts triggers a biochemical reaction that influences every cell in our body. Research shows that peak performers in business, sports, and other areas are highly skilled at mentally picturing outcomes and combining that vision with a resourceful mood state.

The Power of Past Positives

Our prevailing mental models deeply impact our motivation. Because so many of us come from dysfunctional families, we tend to replay past experiences that reinforce our lack of worth rather than those that emphasize our individual worth and greatness. According to John Bradshaw, author of *Homecoming: Reclaiming and Championing Your Inner Child*, during childhood we have recorded as many as twenty-five thousand hours of critical parenting scripts which we play back in adulthood.

In Bright Side seminars, "past positives" are expanded in a way similar to Allison Roe's mental picturing process.

Rediscovery of any past positive can trigger individual, team, or organizational excellence. For example, at the Cleveland manufacturing company Zaclon, employees begin their meetings in a positive, exuberant, and lively manner. Everyone recounts a past positive experience and wears a name tag with a nickname derived from that experience. Employees are even listed in the company phone directory according to these nicknames.

While all this may seem a little corny, these are excellent ways to build spirit, to get people focused on being positive, and to build closer, more intimate relationships. While generating a sense of fun, the focus on past positive experiences helps turn negative thinking into positive energy and motivation, both at work and at home.

Think back in your own life to a time when you had success. It can be any kind of success, like climbing a tree and being able to get right back down, riding your bicycle, getting a good grade on a test, passing driver's education, or being selected for a team. Then think about how you felt.

To the extent that we admit a past experience to be true, we believe it of ourselves today. Practicing rediscovery builds emotional stamina, much in the same way that physical exercise creates endurance. These are the reservoirs we can draw upon when we feel stressed or overwhelmed.

As I recall my Red Ball Jets experience, I feel exuberant. I feel the same sense of accomplishment that I did when I was five years old, even though the events happened nearly forty years ago.

A woman once told me about her childhood in the mountains of Italy, where she learned to trust her ability to travel narrow ledges on a steep mountainside. As a young child, she did this alone by listening to, trusting, and following the encouraging coaching of her mother. She said that memory from her childhood is a significant component of her self-confidence today.

Today, I want you to make a list of your successes. Begin with the small successes of life. Keep adding to this success list throughout the entire day successes that you remember from any time in your life, and, of course, the successes that you create today. At the end of the day, applaud yourself. Be grateful for the successes you have discovered and rediscovered. And tomorrow, get on track and begin the day on a positive note by reading that success list to yourself.

6

Mental Modeling

My childhood was not particularly joyful. Yet I can remember some wonderful, joy-filled experiences as I review my early life. Growing up in Disco, Michigan, I spent a lot of time in the country beer garden. There, I watched the adults drink while I ate pistachios, drank Faygo Red Pop, and danced with my sister Debby and my Aunt Joy.

One hot summer day, as we drove past the beer gardens, an imaginative idea surfaced in my five-year-old mind. I thought to myself, *If farmers can have beer gardens, I can have a pop garden.* When we arrived home, I collected every empty Faygo Red Pop bottle I could find. I found a number of empty beer bottles and brought all of them to my backyard.

I spent the day digging up the backyard, planting empty Faygo bottles and beer bottles. I put water in my watering can and watered the garden. I felt such optimism about my garden! The next morning, filled with excitement and enthusiasm, I ran out to the garden to see what I had. Knowing that it took a summer for a garden to grow, I watered my garden every day, waiting for the pop garden to magically sprout.

The Positive Path

That joyful memory from my childhood taught me precious lessons for my adulthood. Looking back, I can see that it was perhaps my first brush with mental modeling. I had chosen to travel a positive path and believe in my garden despite the negative things others said. Well-meaning but insensitive people told me, "You think too much," or "That's a crazy idea," or "You're too silly." Those comments were later reinforced by an educational system that instilled fear. Despite a family and a culture that created a deeply embedded sense of shame for the alcoholism, abuse, and divorce that existed in my family, even as a child I saw a way out. I could believe in the magic of my garden.

While we often discuss shifting paradigms in the work field, we often forget about the need for shifting our individual mental paradigms. To achieve success in any endeavor, we must actively reshape the mental models we all have that tell us what is possible and not possible about ourselves and about the world. These models so often condition failure. With these arbitrary mental walls in place, deep ruts form in our thinking that lead us to do things as we've always done them and make us deeply resistant to new learning and thus to necessary change.

To knock down these walls, we sometimes must return to methods that we intuitively grasped as helpful at an early age, only to be taught later they were wrong. I was reminded of this lesson when working with a supervisor named Tom Wickwire. He related his experience of being taught to read as a young child. He was taught to read by using a pointer finger, only to be told later that it interfered with reading. As an adult, Tom took a speed-reading course where he was taught once again to use a pointer finger. He likened this contradiction from his childhood to other negative, limiting habits and beliefs we were taught as children.

We must break out and imagine a broader universe of possibilities, as we naturally did as children. The American challenge is to learn to free that child and to rediscover individual giftedness and national greatness. In Japan, children are treated like precious jewels, like treasures. This sharply contrasts with the lack of respect for children we in America often demonstrate. Japanese corporations encourage the five-year-old within in order to cultivate the creativity, optimism, genius, openness, freedom, and flexibility that exists within the child in all of us.

I once spoke at a national meeting with the famous American sociologist Ashley Montagu, who, much to my amazement, presented a film of a child learning to stand and crawling around to explore its environment. The child was utterly joyful, curious, experimental, open, playful, and sensitive. Montagu noted that we are all designed to be like that child—courageous, fearless, and bold.

As a child, I rarely traveled my positive mental paths. They were overgrown with weeds from lack of use. I more often used the negative mental path, creating deep grooves and ruts that were easy to follow and to fall into. Yet, my pop garden proves the potential was always there.

One hot summer day, while on my usual end-of-the-day run, I passed a man who was gardening. "Persevere!" he said. I was grateful for the encouraging remark. And so, on that run I repeated to myself, "Persevere!"

Minutes later, I passed another gardener, who said, "That's too hard to do." I realized I could choose not to believe the negative suggestion made by that second person. We can discard negative suggestions, choosing instead to believe in those that inspire. We can believe in our own ability to succeed.

When I learned to have a child's faith again, I felt so personally empowered! It felt so different from the imprisonment caused by the negative mental path. I began to understand that all my experiences influenced my thinking and behavior. My motivation was determined by my mood state, which I alone could control. And above all, I recognized that God had given me the surging energy of emotional power that builds confidence necessary for the successful undertaking of any task.

Role Models

In addition to recapturing our natural positive instincts from childhood, we can also erect healthy mental models by mimicking good role models.

I've seen time and again how successful people consciously pattern themselves after role models. One example is the Olympic track star Carl Lewis, who claimed to have used the early track records of Jesse Owens to shape his own desire to become the world's fastest runner.

This role-modeling process can take on a life of its own. Jack Kahl, one of my clients, learned leadership techniques from Wal-Mart founder Sam Walton. In turn, Kahl became a model for Gary Trinetti, a self-made entrepreneur who founded his own wholesale landscape-distribution business. Would it be too much to expect that Trinetti will some day become the role model for yet another younger leader?

Role-modeling can run the gamut from mundane items to more vital items. For instance, when I was trying to work out of my depression some years ago, I seized upon one woman I saw who had an especially dynamic smile. She had a great big grin and beautiful teeth that she displayed to the world. And I noticed how she smiled naturally as she talked. For a long time, I pictured this woman smiling. Eventually, I adapted my own smile, but her example helped me immensely.

As a more vital example, I also studied a variety of good speakers over the years, noting what I liked about their approach. I then adapted their strategies where it seemed to fit my own emerging style. Mentors can be those whom we acknowledge as well as others whom we silently use as guides on our voyage of self-discovery. Ultimately, however, we must adapt their examples, not merely copy them. The goal, after all, is to develop our own authentic style. That requires us to summon the courage to first know who we are.

Envisioning (Setting Goals)

We can also erect new mental models by actively envisioning future possibilities and erecting alternate possible selves. This is not unlike setting goals. And you don't have to already be a world-class champion like Allison Roe to picture future success.

Many years ago, a small Japanese manufacturer of motorized bikes had a vision that some might have called unrealistic. After just six years in business, its founder, Soichiro Honda, decided he would set his company's sights on entering and winning the world's most prestigious motorcycle competition, competing for the Tourist Trophy. Honda went on to do just that, sweeping the races in 1961 and later going on to huge success in the world automotive market.

My pop garden is still planted in Disco. Whenever my children and I are in Michigan, they insist on visiting it. It's still buried, never having grown. But for me, it symbolizes what *has* grown—my own childlike spirit and potential for excellence and authenticity.

7

Launching a Spirit of Adventure

My daughter, Maressa, rushed into the house, beaming with excitement. She had returned from a fifth-grade camping trip full of enthusiasm. She said she had just had the most exciting experience of her life.

I immediately stopped what I was doing, curious to know what could produce such rapture in a ten-year-old. Before I had time to ask, Maressa rapidly began talking. Scarcely able to contain her excitement, she explained that the children had explored caves. The fifth-graders lined up at the mouth of the cave. The lone flashlight was held by the child in front. The children had to enter in single file, holding one another's hand, passing on from front to back information about how and where to move. The caves were so tiny and narrow that they could accommodate only the small bodies of children, so the adults were forced to remain at the entrance while the children went on this adventure alone.

Just as they were about to enter one cave, a well-meaning adult asked for a show of hands from the children who thought they might not finish and might want to come back early, so as to position them at the rear of the line. The question immediately piqued my interest. I wondered how the children's responses influenced the outcome. Maressa said a few of the children did raise their hands. When I asked if she had raised her hand, proudly she told me no.

She explained that the cave was dark and narrow, with ankle-deep water in certain places. She described in detail how she and the other children moved in this narrow passage. At a particularly narrow point, she got stuck and was unable to fully hear the directions from the child in front of her. She screamed and tried maneuvering to free herself, but to no avail. She laughed when I asked if she thought about turning back. It never crossed her mind to return. Maybe her sense of adventure gave her the necessary energy, but she was eventually able to free herself as easily as she had become lodged. She beamed with pride. Her energy and spirit fostered such risk-taking.

But I was curious about the children who weren't so optimistic about the adventure at the outset. "Maressa," I asked, "what happened to those children who thought they might return early? Did they?"

"Yes," she replied.

"All of them?"

Once more, she answered yes.

"What about the others?" I inquired. "Did any of the other children return early?"

"No," she said.

What a brilliant example of how our mental picture influences our behavior! A suggestion of doubt from elsewhere produced fear in some of the children and stifled their sense of adventure. As a result, they were afraid to take the risk.

My daughter's experience of several years ago holds lessons for us all. Adventure, that sense that moved Maressa to the most exciting experience of her life, is the very ingredient to success that American industry must cultivate in the '90s. A sense of adventure propels us, frees us. It keeps us on a path of light. It is the adventure of life, energy, fearlessness, vitality, courage, emotion, love, trust, and creativity that can give us the passion to compete at a higher level and provide our customers satisfaction and delight.

It's entirely natural for people to view change with suspicion and discomfort and thus to resist it. That's because change to most people denotes coldness and loneliness. It means the unknown and being out of control. And it raises, perhaps, the suggestion that *I'm not good enough as I am now.*

But time and time again, I have come across heartening examples—from self-directed industry work teams to nontraditional public school classrooms—of people who take the plunge anyway. They often find, to their delight, that with the change they have more fun even as they improve their results. Students can win awards and earn better grades and companies can increase their sales by experimenting with new and better methods.

In Bright Side, we encourage participants to see change as a normal part of life that is necessary for adventure and to realize that the work environment can become a safe place for self-expression and creative freedom.

We suggest continually seeking out bright ideas, even if they come from another industry or country. We encourage reward and recognition for the big and small wins and changes. We encourage respecting all people for what they want to do and be. We believe that no one has all the answers. We set the stage for adventure and discovery by sparking human curiosity and spontaneity. We believe there is no better time than now to commit; as the German poet Goethe describes, commitment yields bold adventure.

> Until one is committed, there is hesitancy,
> the chance to draw back,
> always ineffectiveness.
> Concerning all acts of initiative and creation,
> there is one elementary truth
> the ignorance of which kills countless ideas
> and endless plans:
> That the moment one definitely commits oneself, then
> providence moves too.
> All sorts of things occur to help one
> that would never otherwise have occurred.
> A whole stream of events issues from the decision,
> raising in one's favor all manner of unforeseen

incidents and meetings and material assistance,
which no man could have dreamed would come his way.
Whatever you can do or dream you can,
begin.
Boldness has genius, power, and magic in it.
Begin it now.

Goethe

Five Methods to Unlock the Spirit of Adventure

1. *Novel Tools.* Novel tools are simple objects—such as stars, crayons, clay, and stickers—that engage our creative mind and provide access to our emotions. They enhance our memory by providing a visual anchor. These tools are explained in chapter 14. By breaking stress, helping us control our moods, activating positive memories, and stimulating our brain function, these tools encourage us to venture out.

2. *Playful and Positive Interactive Experience.* Learning is reinforced by active participation. We learn through repetition, utilization, internalization, and reinforcement of lessons. Through interaction, we make learning a part of us. To intellectually understand adventure is vastly different from actively participating in an adventure. Active participation heightens our mood state. We buy into that understanding not because we have gathered the facts, but rather because we have experienced it.

3. *Rediscovery and Enlargement of Past Positives.* As we discussed in chapter 5, remembering a past success breeds more success. It will give us the confidence needed for adventure.

4. *Mental Picturing of Future Positives.* We can envision the successful adventure (see chapter 5), then go out and replicate it.

5. *Trust the Inner Sense of Direction.* Chapter 2 describes the benefits of trusting intuition. Intuition gives us the courage and impetus to do adventurous work.

Building Confidence

Good managers, by bolstering confidence, can lead their teams to better methods. There are no shortcuts. The role of manager changed at the end of this century with the very nature of work itself. Our work is becoming less physical and more cognitive, less material and more spiritual. So leaders must assist their people in solidifying a sense of self-esteem. Confidence is needed for risk-taking.

We can help our children build positive experiences to bolster confidence at very early ages. Gregg Searle—formerly an IBM manager and now an executive with Diebold and its joint venture with IBM, InterBold—helped his ten-year-old daughter build confidence in a subject she was having difficulty with in school. He suggested that whenever she felt tight or anxious she say the word "awesome" and combine it with a fist-hand movement. He also suggested that she anchor-in the correct answers while studying the night before a test by saying "awesome" and moving her fist.

She thought her father silly, but she did as he recommended. The next morning, the day of the test, Searle placed an "Awesome" sticker on her shirt. The outcome? "Awesome!" as she said, as she earned a grade of 100 percent in a subject that had troubled her. In this case, Gregg used a novel tool in order to encourage his daughter to picture a future positive.

Perhaps the enthusiasm with which my daughter tackled the new adventure of exploring caves at the age of ten was similarly encouraged by some earlier lessons. When she was in kindergarten, Maressa brought home a picture she had drawn in school that day. It showed her looking up at a tree and crying. She lamented that she couldn't climb a tree and that other school friends could. I was heartbroken to hear her disappointment and defeat.

I asked her if she ever tried to climb a tree. "No," she responded. Then I asked her how she could possibly know whether she could climb a tree if she had never tried. She looked at me hopefully. I realized my daughter's self-image was limiting her and leaving her, at age five, in a state of near helplessness. I knew, however, that she had brought me a challenge with which I could help her.

Remembering a graceful tree in our front yard that was large but not intimidating, we proceeded outside, where I encouraged her to climb. My own youthful experience of running the race in my Red Ball Jets guided what I said to her. I kept encouraging her until she reached the very top!

"You did it!" I congratulated her. She beamed.

"How do I get down?" she asked. I stopped. How *would* she get down? I knew she could do it. I told her that climbing down is a completely different experience, requiring some serious anticipation. Slowly, she proceeded down. Each step of the way, I told her what a great job she was doing. Oh, how I wanted to grab her and help, but my experience with the Red Ball Jets told me to keep encouraging her. And I did.

Maressa did make it up the tree and down; what a magnificent success she felt! Whenever she is uncertain of a new challenge, I remind her about that tree and tell her, "Yes, you can."

The next picture Maressa drew was one of a jubilant little girl, smiling and climbing. Now, deeply embedded in her mind is an attitude of, *Yes, you can,* not unlike the message of *The Little Engine That Could.* She is confident.

I once spoke at the National Conference for Laughter and Play, where I met Dr. O. Carl Simonton, the author of *Getting Well Again.* A radiologist who specializes in treating cancer, Dr. Simonton used the example of juggling in his presentation. For many years he thought he couldn't juggle because he'd defined juggling as the simultaneous suspension of a number of objects in the air. But eventually he learned that tossing even one object can be considered juggling. And so in this presentation, he passed out marshmallows for people to juggle.

He said the whole secret to juggling was not focusing on the catch, because that leads to fear. Rather, he said, focus on the toss, which builds a sense of confidence. I want to suggest to you that same kind of thinking pattern in other endeavors—focus on the toss and not on the catch. Focus more on the opportunity or the possibility than the problem. To learn to juggle we must first make hundreds of mistakes.

As we consider children exploring caves, we see that their joy, experimentation, and enthusiasm propelled them to a desired outcome. The results are increased team participation, increased creativity, and heightened mental energy—a true sense of spirit and fun.

8

Doubt or Belief?

Celebrating the individual occurs in many intriguing forms. At Manco, Inc., a Cleveland-based vendor of weather stripping, mailing supplies, and tape, the monthly ESOP (Employee Stock Ownership Plan) meeting brings together all Manco partners (employees) for one to two hours, at an estimated cost of eight thousand dollars per meeting. Fun and spirit are high as the meeting begins with recognition and awards. One of the meetings I attended, sponsored by production, created the excitement of a baseball game, complete with peanuts, popcorn, and uniforms. In this environment, the production partners communicate information about their process and the responsibilities of the team and the team members.

A new tradition has evolved at Manco—the annual Duck Challenge. Adapted from an idea used by Sam Walton, yet born of chairman and CEO Jack Kahl's understanding that being outrageous sets one apart, this ritual symbolizes breaking out of the box of our long conditioned sense of conformity. It's Manco's annual celebration of the year's successes. The first year, Kahl was the lone swimmer in the duck pond in front of Manco's headquarters. Last year, four hundred Manco friends joined in the general festivities, myself included. With a trace of snow on the ground from the previous day, forty of the four hundred, myself included, braved the unusually frigid October temperatures and swam bravely across the fifty-foot-long duck pond.

A little nervous about speaking later that day to the sizable Manco audience, I was calmed when I realized there was a thirteen-year-old girl among us. She won my heart! This was a very special girl who was scheduled to speak about her incredible commitment to our environment.

Melissa Poe, at age nine, watched the TV series *Highway to Heaven,* in which Michael Landon played an angel bringing heavenly good to earth. A particular show triggered her fear about the environment. Supported by her mother, Melissa wrote a letter to President Bush. She was frustrated in receiving a form-letter response, but she persevered. She called a billboard company and enlisted its help. "Dear Mr. President" billboards were donated in Washington, D.C., where she hoped the president would see them. The response from those who saw the billboards became the impetus for her new environmental club, which she named Kids F.A.C.E. (Kids for a Clean Environment).

Melissa's mom, Trish, encouraged and supported Melissa. She says, "Melissa's plea to the president to not ignore her letter struck me. Our biggest mistake as adults is minimizing our children's fears and concerns. We don't give credibility to them or their thinking. When we channel their fears into an activity, we encourage them to try things. That physical action of doing something contributes to their mental well-being.

"Both Melissa and I know what we are doing is guided by the hand of God. Melissa felt God was speaking to her when she watched *Highway to Heaven.* It is an awakening for us to trust what happens or doesn't happen as part of God's master plan." In 1990, after Melissa's efforts earned her an appearance on the *Today* show, she began receiving letters, to which she personally responded. The mail and the requests for projects and information required an increasing family commitment of time and resources.

Trish Poe says, "I saw the big picture—my inexperience and the need for financial support. I didn't have an answer. I went to sleep praying, 'Please help, Lord.' That morning at 3:00 A.M., I awoke from a sound sleep to a loud, booming, forceful voice, *Call Wal-Mart.* God spoke to me about Wal-Mart."

She wrote a letter to Mr. Sam at Wal-Mart. Two weeks later, Wal-Mart telephoned, asking, "How can we help you with Kids F.A.C.E.?" The company flew Melissa and her mom to Arkansas for the Wal-Mart advisory board meeting. Melissa told them her experience.

Since that time, Melissa has spoken to many executives and dignitaries. Kids F.A.C.E. has grown to an international membership of over one hundred thousand. Wal-Mart has supported it with millions of printings and mailings each year, as well as with other financial support.

Melissa's adult dream may include running for president—to make a difference in the world. She already has made one!

Manco has also funded Kids F.A.C.E. Manco is spearheading the Ambassador Program, in which high school students provide role-models and leadership for younger children. The program has started at St. Edwards High School in Cleveland. Thirty high school kids have now helped sixty younger kids clean parks, test water, and run science experiments. Melissa's newest Kids F.A.C.E. goal is to create a children's forest. She and classmate Courtney Collins and children from Oregon have presented a proposal to the National Forest Service to designate certain areas in national parks for children to adopt, explore, and plant trees in.

Even today, Melissa says, people actually do not believe what she has done. Doubt or belief? It's amazing the difference belief will produce. It is a choice.

Kids F.A.C.E. started with one nine-year-old child's concern, was supported by encouraging, believing people, and ultimately guided by God's hand. All you have to do is ask. Believe. Do. Be persistent. Never give up. As Trish Poe has often prayed, "Please help, Lord."

In similar fashion, most companies that want to become leaders in their industries come to realize that a vision of what might be possible is their first priority. At Timken, a Canton, Ohio-based manufacturer, some people have nurtured the quite untraditional vision of allowing the unionized work force more flexible work schedules. One supervisor asked her employees when they wanted to work, which is quite radical in a unionized workplace. Others are taking the initiative to establish a more focused approach to customer delight. As a company, Timken has a simple vision—it wants to be the best manufacturing company in the world. Not just in the U.S., but the best anywhere. And with those targets in sight, who's to say they won't get there?

9

Let Us Reacquaint Ourselves with Youth

Companies can succeed and individuals can be happy when they return to earlier, more natural ways of approaching the world, the way we once did as children.

Consider some examples that have buoyed my spirits. Their particulars are different, as are their environments, but they share deeper parallels. They each demonstrate that by returning to youthful approaches even deeply entrenched methods can change.

InterBold, a manufacturer of automated teller machines, or ATMs, was formed in 1990 through the combination of the ATM components of two old, successful companies that had previously competed head-to-head in the business—International Business Machines and Diebold.

IBM, of course, is primarily a computer manufacturer. It has been in business since before World War I. Diebold, a venerable manufacturer of safes and security systems, is even older. It achieved its reputation by producing safes that survived intact during the Great Chicago Fire of 1871 and the catastrophic San Francisco earthquake of 1906.

The companies' ATM divisions were combined in the fall of 1990 and immediately wanted to build momentum by introducing a new ATM product line. But they wanted to avoid a typical mistake in product development, says InterBold chairman and Diebold executive vice-president Gregg Searle, who spent eighteen years with IBM. "There is often a tendency to build new products without talking to customers about their needs. When you do that, you can develop a cure for which there's no known disease."

So the new organization spent a year soliciting information from hundreds of customers in banking and related industries around the world. The dominant theme that emerged from this research was that ATM purchasers were tired of paying for machines that rapidly became obsolete. Perhaps even worse, when the time came for reinstallation of a new model, the newer machine was often of different dimensions than the previous one, thus necessitating costly facility reconfiguration. The market, in short, was asking for a system that could be incrementally upgraded, at a lower cost, with less down time.

"Up until then," Searle explains, "manufacturers of these machines designed them like they would a dishwasher. So the useful life span was generally about five years, if you wanted to keep up with the technology."

This time, InterBold summoned its engineers, who were used to getting their marching orders in highly detailed, technical parameters. "What we gave them instead were a list of adjectives that described customers' needs. That really changed the paradigm," Searle says.

The method for organizing work teams to design, build, and then unveil the new product was similarly radical. "We basically created what you could call boundaryless teams for product development and the new product announcement. People from engineering, marketing, advertising, and manufacturing worked together," he says. Without regard to seniority and rank, the best and the brightest from each area of the company were assembled into fluid work teams whose composition ebbed and flowed as the work demanded. These teams were given authority by senior management to bring in other employees as "expert witnesses" to add their technical input as needed. "To be quite honest with you, [this latitude] was so foreign to them that for a while, they kept running things up the flagpole to senior management," says Searle.

What resulted from all the activity, in the fall of 1991—just one year after the joint venture was born—was a new family of products that included upgrade kits to allow customers to keep their current hardware in place while still keeping abreast of the improving technology, at half the cost or less of a new machine.

The unveiling was carried off with style. Company advertising and marketing people had become familiar with the project from its inception and thus were ready with a unique marketing push. "We figured that if the advertising and public relations people really knew what we were doing, if they got a visceral sense of what we were trying to do and what the customer wanted—they could really promote it," says Searle.

The new i Series product line and upgrade kits have been tremendously well-received. "We've shipped thousands," says Searle. And in the process, InterBold hasn't merely taken business away from competitors but has helped grow the total market, convincing more buyers that they need upgradeable ATMs.

The effect on InterBold employees who participated in the product design, manufacture, and launch has been noticeable as well. "It was the most liberating, creative thing for them," says Searle. "I don't think all these people have ever felt so connected to one another. Generally, in a large corporation, you work on a small piece of the operation, and down the road it all gets pulled together. And maybe you're aware of how that comes together and maybe you're not."

Searle notes that in some industries, this flexible management approach wouldn't be considered radical. "But in our industry, no one had ever done this," he says. "You can get pretty ingrained in your thinking when you've been in business since the Civil War." The company's flexible approach in some ways mimics a child's fresh problem-solving patterns.

American public schools are also deeply ingrained environments where change is enormously difficult and following in old, well-established grooves is easy. As the quality expert W. Edwards Deming liked to say, schools have a way of squelching the individual. And Becky Yates Shorb could have followed those grooves comfortably into retirement.

For twenty-five years, the last twenty-three at the same high school, Becky has been an art teacher in the Maryland countryside near the presidential retreat of Camp David, just a few miles from the Civil War battlefield of Gettysburg. Though she constantly searches out new ideas and approaches for her classroom, she admits to having become burned-out recently. "The past several years have been miserable," she says. Her schedule was full of administrative duties that broke her concentration on teaching. She was beginning to feel undervalued in the system. "There's a wealth of untapped knowledge among teachers," she says.

But she wasn't defeated by forces beyond her control, choosing instead to try a new approach in her own classroom. Like Searle, she envisioned an environment in which people could learn new ways of doing things by freeing themselves to stretch for higher goals. Then she supported that vision with strong underlying people-centered values.

She introduced Bright Side concepts in class after coming across an earlier edition of this book. She brought bubbles and jacks, kaleidoscopes and multicolored balls to the classroom. (See chapter 18.) And she erected a huge sign over her door, welcoming students to the bright side. She plans in the future to take her students out behind the school to build mud pies, a classic youthful pastime.

And the students' reaction? "They loved it," Becky says. "Especially the bubbles. For me, it was like watching little kids getting their bubbles for the first time." And her colleagues have taken note. She has begun sharing her new methods with them.

In the meantime, although her school system was not traditionally a highly rated one, her students have lately recorded some conspicuous successes. One is scheduled to have her artwork displayed in the state capitol, and others are having their work displayed at a state horse show and reproduced on the cover of a booklet for a county science fair.

Becky recently heard her school system's new superintendent interviewed on a radio call-in program, where he discussed the possibility of dropping old, ineffective school programs. She responded by writing him a note in which she offered the opinion that there's little use changing programs without addressing underlying stale attitudes. Shrewdly cutting to the heart of the matter, she says, "It's not so much the material you teach but the environment you're creating."

At Original Copy Centers, the inner child is released at the company's traditional Halloween parties. Great thought goes into creating Halloween costumes, even to the extent of making costumes that resemble Original Copy Center's product—black-and-white copies in sizes ranging from the traditional 8 1/2 x 11 paper up through all the other copy sizes that they provide.

At Forest City Enterprise, a real estate development company, experimentation with new ideas for marketing budget meetings was encouraged through a mailing of "fun packs." These fun packs were comprised of a balloon helicopter, color pens, a mini-puzzle, a runner's cap, chocolates, and a squirt gun. Forest City wanted their marketing directors to consider the mundane things they have to do for budget cutbacks and look at them differently. Marketing directors came to budget meetings more open and ready for these reductions. They were eager to discuss new approaches to their challenges for the year, which included standard items like how to get customers to shop. The tools served as a metaphor, a visual bridge, to the importance of what was being discussed that day—fresh approaches for reducing costs. The unusual items in the fun packs helped anchor ideas in the memory, since experts estimate that we remember 85 percent of what we see.

Those same characteristics that come naturally to kids—spontaneity, creativity, inventiveness, fearlessness, authenticity, a sense of joy and of fun and of truth—offer the seeds of hope to us as adults. If we have any hope of moving out of the tired rituals of habit, we must learn to become childlike, though not childish. As the Bible says: "I tell you the truth, unless you change and become like little children, you will never enter the kingdom of heaven" (Matt. 18:3).

All across this country, creative, risk-taking leaders in every imaginable walk of life are emerging one by one to reintroduce these powerful elements back into the classroom, the home, the executive suite, and the shop floor.

These elements that breed good leadership are the very same characteristics that work teams and families and other groups of collaborative strivers will need in order to bring together love, work, and play into a seamless web.

By whatever means it's accomplished, when we return to our more youthful state of mind, we become better problem-solvers. We're more apt to experiment with new solutions to old problems. And that will generally result in pleasing your customers.

Part 3

Model Bright Side People

In the following section, you'll learn about Thomas Edison's knack for inventiveness. Then you'll meet a contemporary trio of the most insightful, original thinkers on management. And they're no mere theorists—Jack Kahl, Nancy Vetrone, and Jim Krimmel have founded their own companies from less-than-ideal beginnings. They have sent their organizations down paths that you might call unique. Their names, for the most part, aren't famous, but their philosophies are refreshing and insightful.

Good leadership is an elusive mix of traits. It combines a firm grasp of the technical details with a handle on the more intuitive, human skills of getting along with others and expanding their horizons. Good leaders, as the accompanying diagram suggests, know how to inspire others by encouraging them to break past their self-imposed limits and release those fears that halt success.

Like Edison, these modern managers—all of whom I'm proud to say have been my clients—encountered deep challenges in their personal lives as well as their entrepreneurial careers. Jim Krimmel recounts waking at night, shortly after purchasing his company from DuPont, from a nightmare that his flesh was being torn from his body. Jack Kahl's confidence was nearly shattered after a young employee's unsupervised inexperience nearly brought his company to the brink of disaster. And not long before founding her spectacularly successful company, the newly divorced Nancy Vetrone was forced to use a picnic cooler as a refrigerator for her four children for over a year.

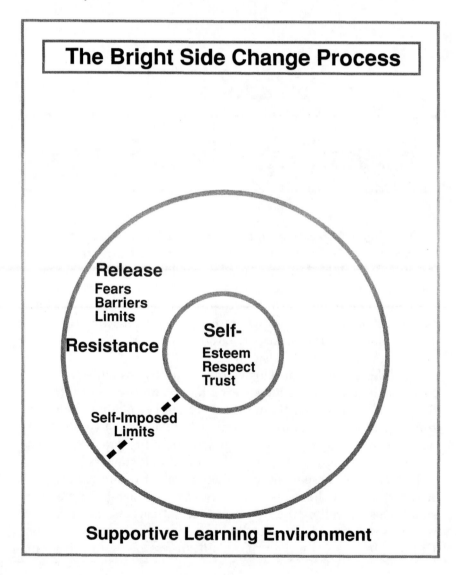

The Bright Side Change Process

Release
Fears
Barriers
Limits

Resistance

Self-
Esteem
Respect
Trust

Self-Imposed
Limits

Supportive Learning Environment

But there is a deep curiosity, a restlessness, and an unwillingness to succumb to the odds that spin a thread through each of their lives and through the lives of all great leaders. Kahl remembers being a mischievous youngster, "always taking chances." That put him in good stead later.

Perhaps the most important trait most good leaders seem to share is a penchant for lifelong learning. They are driven by a spirit that self-effacingly admits that they don't have all the answers. Only a truly strong leader such as Jim Krimmel would admit that his new employees used to approach him to ask how they should do something, only to be told: "I don't know how you do that or what you should do. What do you think? What are we trying to accomplish?" (See chapter 13.) His latter question, I suspect, was the true beginning of the organization's learning and the foundation of its success.

10

A Better Way

"If there is a better way to do it, find it." You might think that statement arises from a '90s quality team, perhaps inspired by the Japanese. In fact, it comes from America's great inventor and entrepreneur, Thomas Edison.

Americans don't necessarily need to turn to Japan to find the keys to our greatness, because they're embedded in our heritage and within each of us. In fact, *inventiveness* is probably the best word to describe Americans of a century ago. Inventiveness was our national habit. Even Abraham Lincoln was moved to observe that every time an American family had a baby, the family would look for ways to improve the cradle.

Edison ran thousands and thousands of experiments—fifty thousand with the alkaline battery alone. Instead of focusing on a mistake, he would say, "Now I know what not to do the next time." He lived a full and productive life. At his death, he was a wealthy man and had amassed more than one thousand patents. His keys to greatness? Self-belief. Determination. Resiliency. As a very young child, he was curious, spontaneous, creative, inventive, fearless, and filled with joy and passion. These are all qualities we naturally exhibit as young children and that leaders would like to emulate and inspire in others.

When Edison was three, his curiosity led him to an experiment. He sat on duck, chicken, and goose eggs to see if his own warmth would hatch them. We don't know the outcome—whether the young inventor got eggs on his pants or even if the eggs hatched—but that childhood story clearly demonstrates his spirit for adventure.

His mother nurtured his individuality and encouraged his inventiveness. In contrast, his father had no tolerance for the boy's experimentation, often severely disciplining him. When Edison was about ten, he experimented with matches and straw and burned down the family barn. His father called together all the townspeople to watch as he publicly spanked his son with a strap in the town square. The boy received similar treatment from his schoolmaster, who called him dumb and said he couldn't learn.

The great inventor later said that at one point he almost believed his father and schoolmaster, that he wouldn't amount to anything. But he made a decision. He chose not to believe his father but rather his mother, who believed in him and in his potential. Throughout his life, Edison never again was constrained by the boundaries painted by the harshness of his father and his teacher.

In fact, he continuously broke out of boundaries. He once hired a mathematician to calculate the volume of a lightbulb. Struggling with the concepts and formulas, the mathematician, growing frustrated, gave up. Edison said, "There is a better way; there is an easier way." He broke off the tip of the bulb, filling it with water and emptying it into a beaker for measurement. He trusted his childlike curiosity and his intuition.

He had a great sense of humor. When he was ready to test the phonograph he had developed, instead of recording something self-important, he recorded the children's nursery rhyme, "Mary Had a Little Lamb." He put that same phonograph under the bed in his guest bedroom after recording on it the message, "In one hour you will meet your God." While a houseguest was asleep one night, Edison sneaked into the room and turned the machine to full volume while he hid behind a door. His friend awoke with a start, panicked, and ran out of the room.

The characteristics that Edison personified are those same qualities that leaders need today. We need leaders to inspire and nurture. Edison liked to say that his purpose was to make life easier and more enjoyable for others. Edison made failure a friend. His laboratory was a learning organization. Yet, he looked beyond his needs, driven by his purpose to serve his "customers." We as leaders should be doing that too.

Sam Walton was also, as Edison, a lifelong student. A former Wal-Mart vice-president, Ron Loveless, once explained to me that when a competitor was doing well, Walton would study its tactics. Never satisfied with the status quo, Walton constantly looked for a better way.

"It isn't always easy to have a mindset of a learner. Even if the boss is wrong, there is something to learn—greater knowledge or self-knowledge," says Loveless. He recalls being promoted to district manager for Wal-Mart and having to report to a regional manager he did not like. The manager had criticized him. After much soul-searching, Loveless determined to try to get along with him. He told his boss, at first sarcastically and later genuinely, that he appreciated what he was being taught. He later realized that because he made the effort to get along with the manager, the manager was able to teach him a lot. Loveless came to acknowledge that he hadn't previously been running the stores as well as he could.

These two men accomplished more as a team than they ever could have individually. In four years, they turned their district from the worst in the chain to the best. The principle: We can learn from anyone. And it worked for Ron Loveless.

Loveless first began working for Wal-Mart by assembling bicycles for a store opening. He invented a system for putting together the first bike and used it on the next forty. He says that system is still the best. From that humble beginning, he became vice-president of Wal-Mart and executive vice-president and general manager of Sam's Club.

As Dr. Martin Luther King, Jr. wrote: "If a man is called a street-sweeper, he should sweep streets even as Michelangelo painted, or Beethoven composed music, or Shakespeare wrote poetry. He should sweep streets so well that all the hosts of heaven and earth will pause to say, *Here lived a great streetsweeper who did his job well.*"[3] This is the better way.

11

Darkness before the Dawn

An Interview with Jack Kahl,
Chairman and CEO of Manco, Inc.

Jack Kahl, Jr., chairman and CEO of Manco, Inc., began his tenure with the company in 1963. In 1966 he became general manager, and on June 1, 1971, he purchased the business. When Kahl joined the firm in 1963, annual sales totaled $83,000. Under his leadership, sales grew to $5 million in 1978 and have recently surpassed the $100 million mark.

Manco is a consumer-market vendor of weather-stripping, mailing supplies, and Duck brand adhesive tape. Manco's trademark is a colorful family of Manco ducks. The theme of the cuddly and colorful Manco family of ducks is evident throughout Manco: it's on the Spirit (How High Can We Climb) Award and on greeting cards for all seasons and holidays; there are Manco duck costume characters, Manco plush duck dolls and toys, the Manco Ducktails Newsletter, and the Manco Duck Challenge Swim; and there are even pictures of ducks on machines, towmotors, and offices throughout the company.

Kahl talks about how his childhood shaped his life and how he empowers his employees to achieve. As I start my interview, he tells me he has just sent a check to a woman whose husband, an employee at Manco, was killed in a fire. She was at the Manco Christmas party with her two surviving children (she lost another boy in the fire). Her eight-year-old boy, who was in the fire, was there in a burn suit all the way up to his neck, hidden because it was under his clothes.

"He put out his little hand," Kahl says. "He couldn't shake hands with his right hand, so I had to shake his left hand. And I'm thinking, whoa boy, what a year this little guy had, and you wouldn't know it! He was smiling and happy even though he had burn scars all over the side of his face." Jack was quite taken by his courage.

The mother is out of a job and needed help, so the Manco people collected the money they usually use for a gift for Kahl and instead gave her a gift certificate for $270. "We're looking to see if we can find a job for her here," Kahl says. "In the meantime, she needs a Christmas. I was once in that kind of position, a long time ago.

"When we were kids in Cleveland, we were on welfare, so Christmas was somebody else's hand-me-downs wrapped up, which was fine. At the time it was great. Had it not been for education, my father's hard work, and my desire to improve, I still might be down on West Twenty-fifth Street.

"I think back a lot of times, had I not gotten out of there to a better neighborhood, there's no telling where I would have gone. Two of my buddies were both dead before they were eighteen years old. We weren't bad guys, but we were hanging around with people in a bad environment. I was a mischievous youngster. I'm always taking chances.

"When I was ten, I was in a gang. My brother and I were the leaders. We had all kinds of great buddies. We would shake the bums under the High Level Bridge, wake them up, make them chase us, do all kinds of things. We were looking for things to do. There was an empty building and we decided to break a window and see what was in there. We found old pieces of glass that nobody wanted. We took them home. Mom beat the heck out of me and told me to take that back. She was frightened to death. Then I knew it was wrong. We didn't know at that time that what we did was wrong."

Jack's father had TB. Because TB was misunderstood at that time, professionals put him in a sanitarium. Jack's early recollections of his father are of seeing him in a fourth-story window. He would throw money from a coin purse down to Jack. He had TB three times—the first time for a year, the next time for a year-and-a-half, and then again for a year-and-a-half. The third time doctors performed an operation called a lobectomy, in which they cut out the diseased part of the lung. That finally cured him.

"During that time we moved from the old neighborhood where my parents grew up to the West Twenty-fifth Street projects. Those were tough times. A lot of relatives looked down on us because we were on welfare. I remember those things. But there were some wonderful relatives that always brought potatoes and ice cream and took me to the circus and made me feel good about myself.

"My mom was a jewel. She said as the oldest boy, I needed to get a job. We needed money. I was seven. I was riding my sled one day, and I saw this guy with a paper route. I knocked on his window. And he said, 'What do you want, kid?' And I said, 'Mister, I want a job.'

"'How old are you?' he asked. I told him, and he said, 'Why do you want a job?' I told him.

"He said, 'Well, you go around the projects and if you can find any people who will take the paper, I'll give you a route.' So I went all over, knocking on doors, and I found an old lady on the fourth floor who said she wanted a subscription. Then I went to the Harbor Inn Bar, which is still in business, where all the sailors used to come from all around the world. I rounded up another customer there. So the guy gave me a paper route with two customers. I kept it for about two years. When I left I had twenty-two customers."

Jack swears his wanderlust started then. "I used to go down to the bar and drop that paper off at the Harbor Inn. The sailors would put me up on the bar stool, and they would talk, kid around, and buy me a pop, and I would hear these guys talk in different languages, and I was always taken by it. I always wanted to know more. I liked it. They were real kind to me. My whole impression of the world was made first by these people.

"Then I would leave and go in the projects. Big guys intimidated us little ones. You are rated by how tough you are. So that was my early background."

Then Kahl's dad came home. He worked for American Greetings Corporation as the chairman's secretary. The chairman had to approve every verse that was written. As secretary, Jack's father started making comments on verses. Soon he was checking verses. Then he was working in the verse department. Finally, he became head of the verse department!

Kahl's father started selling real estate at night part-time to make more money. He couldn't get American Greetings to give him a big enough raise, so he did something Jack admires him for—he quit. "We had six kids living in the projects, and we were off welfare but still very poor. Yet, he left that job. I'll never forget that. He went on straight commission in real estate to sell full time because he was making more money part time at nights and weekends than he was at American Greetings.

"He never stopped. He worked his tail off seven days a week and educated six kids. He got enough to buy our first house out near the airport, with apple orchards and woods. It cost $9,500. It had an old brick driveway, old-fashioned sink, and glass-covered doors, but every rug had a throw rug over it because there was a hole underneath it. The garage fell down two months after we moved in. My mother cried for three months when she moved in. She wanted to move back to the projects. It was a terrible house. But we kids loved it. We had polliwog ponds in the backyard. We put in a driveway and a new garage."

By that time Jack was working two jobs and going to school. "My brother and sister were working, too. My mother always gave us our own bank accounts. She always said this was our money and gave us credit for what we did. If she needed something, we'd go to the bank and get some money because the family needed it. We also had people who were great friends, who weren't even relatives but whom we called uncles and aunts, who just came over and helped. I especially recall that at Christmastime. Those people taught me real generosity. The root system of all this came from my mother, my father, and family."

This background gave Jack desire, a sense of achievement, and the recognition that comes from work. He always had a buck in his pocket. When he was in construction, he always put 80 percent of his earnings in the bank. He always had control of himself and his environment. "Work has given me a lot," Jack says.

Jack's father expected good grades and had very strict standards. "At times, he could be so expecting, so demanding, it made me shy because it took away my willingness to risk certain things. I had to overcome that shyness in this business."

Part of the reason Jack started a small and manageable business was to get out of the limelight of downtown Cleveland. He had worked for one year and had not liked it. Then he discovered Manco. As it started getting bigger he was afraid that he couldn't handle what was coming. Business was going to grow, but he felt it was going to grow past him, that he was going to have to get out of chairing because he didn't have the personality to handle the job. "I started reading books on it and started pretending to others that I was capable of it, even though I didn't believe it on the inside. Now it's easy to share that because now I know I can do it. But in 1981, I didn't think so. I was looking like it, talking like it, acting like it, but I didn't believe it for a minute."

Jack owed the bank about $4 million, signed for by him personally, but he felt in reasonably good control because he had people around him who he thought were in control as well. His downfall came in the place he least suspected—a fine young man who was brilliant at finance but terrible at delegating. This man had four people under him, but he was falling farther and farther behind. One night, in front of his young staff, he resigned. The reason? The books were six months in arrears. He was completely befuddled and buried in work, way out of control financially.

"It was a total shock," Jack says. "My whole security system—everything—was endangered. I was completely broken in spirit because I thought I had bankrupted. It was far worse in my mind than it was in reality. I wasn't mad at the young man. I held myself responsible for being so stupid that I had not seen it coming. It was the darkest single moment of my existence. I lost a great deal of confidence in myself and my judgment. I got some counseling and found out a lot of people go through what I did. Slowly, ever so slowly, I started rebuilding a little faith in myself."

Nobody at Manco knew how deep the shock went. Everybody knew Jack was exhausted, but nobody knew how psychologically frightened he had been. He took anxiety pills, mostly because, as he says, "I lacked faith in my own self-control and my own feelings." That went on for two years, from 1981 to 1983.

How did he come out of this period? "That stuff teaches you a lot. I went out and started getting real smart people. The need to bring in people from professional service areas who could see the big picture became obvious to me. So I went and got Arthur Andersen (an accounting firm) and Calfee Halter (a law firm) and started to pay for what I wanted. I had to break relationships to do that. I had to ask others to step aside and act as advisers rather than doers. I kept the friendships but changed the people who did the business. So there was a lot of emotional stuff going on. I pulled through by reading, trying, and not quitting. That was the biggest thing."

I ask Jack about the time he stood alone to do the Wal-Mart cheer. He had attended the Wal-Mart shareholders meeting in the Arkansas field house. "It was extraordinary," he says. "I went to the Saturday morning meeting, and I was sitting in the audience with about nine hundred people—among them Wal-Mart associates and Wall Street financial analysts.

"Sam Walton was in better style than ever because he was entertaining the Wall Street group. Saturday morning meetings are fun, but this one was extraordinary fun while getting the job done, too. It was so much fun and so uplifting. I got so motivated sitting there that when David Glass, the president, asked if anybody had any questions, I raised my hand. I said, 'I don't have a question, I have to tell you something.' Before you knew it, I was up the aisle, on stage, talking and telling all the Wal-Mart people what I thought of them, how much fun it was to come down there and work and share time with them. I said, 'I want to lead you guys in a Wal-Mart cheer.' Sam Walton said, 'Well, let's give him some help.' So he got the fourteen regional managers out of the front row, put them behind me, and we started doing it. That was the first time in my entire life that I ever got up in front of a big group of people like that. I had thought about doing it hundreds of times, but I never did. I never had the guts to do it."

When asked why he did it, Jack responds, "I was motivated to go beyond myself! Isn't it an amazing thing? It breaks through the fear. You break it by doing it. There's a sign back at Manco from Joseph Conrad. Everyone around here knows it's one of my favorites. It says, 'Facing up to your worst fears is the best thing that you can do. Look at it, deal with it.'"

We discuss Sam Walton's motivational strategies, and I ask Kahl how he motivates people. He answers, "With open information, straightforward talk, and communication. We made some changes. We took the most people-oriented people we had and put them in charge of managing people. We took the technical people who were good with machines and put them in charge of machines.

"For example, we have a twenty-one-year-old employee here named Scotty. They were going to let him go because he was always tardy. Then I learned that he had a paper route in the morning that made him tardy. But they were always yelling at him, never praising him."

Scotty is an extraordinary young person. Jack tells me Scotty is a high school grad. He delivers newspapers to two hundred customers before he comes to work at Manco. He hung a quality-standard sign over his machine listing the eight things that can be wrong with a roll of gift wrap. The sign also shows people where to put rejects. He has a picture of the Manco Duck he drew on a piece of corrugated paper saying, "We gotta take care of our customers."

Kahl says, "I went to his supervisor and told him this kid has talent to be supervisor in two years or less if only he wants to be. I want to help him. I told him, 'Tell me what you want to do with your life and I'll try to help you get there. But first you have to know where you want to go.' I told him to look at our plant manager. He only has a high school education! He started out as a beverage-store manager; then he started here part time. But look how far he's come! Also, I told him to look at Wal-Mart executive Dean Sanders. He's a high-school graduate, too, but he'll probably be Wal-Mart president or CEO one day.

"Now Scott has been attending our Thursday meetings by choice," Jack says. "I'm sure he'll go far."

Jack got the idea for Manco's Thursday meetings from seeing the success of the Wal-Mart Saturday morning meetings. He says the value of the meeting is communication. Sam Walton adds energy and fun, with cheers, jumping jacks, running in place, group activities, and togetherness. Besides simply being fun, these things keep everyone's attention focused on the subject because their blood is running and their minds are alert.

Kahl says what he thinks is important is the communication of things to the group that never gets done between nine and five because nobody ever has time to get that many people together. He started meetings because Manco could not communicate information through the ranks as fast as the rate of change in the marketplace.

The idea of meetings was negatively received until the first meeting. It's been positive from that day on. The time was changed to Thursdays instead of Saturdays. People liked it. They discovered friends in other departments. Social bonds formed that haven't broken, and a lot of things took place that Jack is sure are not happening in other companies because other companies aren't having meetings.

The meetings are organized around Peter Drucker's principle: "Remember, here's how to run a business: Buy cheap, package well, and sell dear." The meeting starts with *sell dear,* so the salesmen report. Then it's *buy cheap,* so the operations and purchasing people give a report on raw materials. *Package well* is the marketing people, so the merchandising and marketing presentations are made. Afterwards, some employees go out for a few beers, and rookies are invited to join them. People bond, friendships are made, a beer or two is had, and the company keeps getting tighter. Kahl attributes the bond to openness, information, feedback, and willingness to try to find and celebrate the positive. "Celebrate the positive, and then that allows you to go after the negative in a fast-changing business," he says.

Many business people take a negative approach. "They don't and won't risk their feelings and their hearts," Kahl says. "They come in with a brusque, businesslike face and a gray-flannel-suit mind. They walk in and give you analytical fluff up to your ears. They give you another number and talk head-count talk. They say we have to cut heads. That's an easy way to distance yourself—use big-man talk. I don't want big-man talk in this company." Jack at times experiences intense fear that is driven by not wanting to let people go. "There's no need for letting people go if you do things right," he says.

Manco has summer concerts around the pond. They bring hospital speakers in to help with stress. They improved the weight room. They offer college reimbursement, new office furniture, family things: Cleveland Indians special family day, kids' coloring contests, smoke alarms, a Christmas party, a Thanksgiving turkey. They gave employees potted plants for the Earth Day celebration. They added park benches around the pond. They planted trees on Arbor Day and sent everyone home with a tree. They have Santa Claus visit at the annual Christmas party. Every year they have a lottery: Kahl gives five hundred dollars of his own money to the person who comes closest to guessing the year's total sales figures. They are an ESOP (Employee Stock Ownership Plant), which makes every single person a partner and owner of Manco. They operate as a family. "We share the risks and we share the rewards," Kahl says.

They even had a contest. Kahl says, "We needed to reduce our inventory. Many times people are afraid to discuss problems, but I wanted to humanize the problem and make fun of it so that people were not afraid to bring it up. So I had a contest to see who could come up with the most clever way to name this problem so we could deal with it. The winner was a young man who had just become a new father. His mother works here, too. He nicknamed the inventory-control problem SCUD, or Still Collecting Unwanted Dust. Isn't that great? I really liked his creativity! I gave him two hundred dollars from my own pocket for that."

Manco has a bell that they ring whenever there's good news. Jack thinks it helps employee morale. "The bell is also rung when I talk too much at a meeting," he adds.

The Manco Duck is a popular mascot. People asked to have duck symbols and signs for their own decoration, and it spread. "I love it," says Kahl. "It's like a barometer, and if people want to display it, it means they like the place. To me, it says they're giving their hearts and souls to this place. It's also a sign of warmth and fun, almost like a Walt Disney atmosphere! A Manco rep carries a plush Manco Duck doll in his car. This same man is receiving the Spirit Award for energizing a client meeting with the Manco cheer.

"Work needs to be fun, both for me and the people who work here. You spend your whole life here. You can make it a prison, but I think it must be enjoyable. You can't focus on the bottom line. The bottom line is a result, not a cause. The numbers are phenomenal, but I don't get driven by numbers. I've read the book recently on Andrew Carnegie and great American entrepreneurs, and not one of them got success by a set of numbers. They got it because they believed in themselves and saw a vision of something bigger than anybody else saw, and they were busy building big enough buildings to house their dreams."

Jack concludes, "You need numbers, but I don't make decisions from the numbers. I get the best people, I create a good environment, and I try to get out of their way so they can do their jobs. I encourage them and try to be part of it myself. The profit is the end result that keeps getting better. You can't do it the opposite way."

12

The Bright Side at Work

An Interview with Nancy Vetrone, Founder of Original Copy Centers, Inc.

Nancy Vetrone is the founder of Original Copy Centers, Inc., which has since been purchased by Copy America. It was the first print-for-pay copy center in Ohio and has been recognized as the largest copy center in North America by *Quick Printing* magazine. It has customers around the world.

Original Copy specializes in the reproduction of books and manuals on an overnight or short turnaround basis. It can also produce one million letter-size impressions overnight. Vetrone's business has been on the *Inc. 500* list of fastest-growing private companies in America for four years in a row, from 1986 to 1989. She has been recognized by Ernst & Young as "Entrepreneur of the Year."

Vetrone's company has taken the mundane commodity service of making photocopies and turned it into a high-tech, profitable business of black-on-white document management services for the corporate market. Its goal is to help offices manage the proliferation and reproduction of documents—simply put, to help people communicate.

The company is also a Bright Side client. I recently interviewed Vetrone about her company, herself, and the value of Bright Side ideals in business.

As we began talking, Nancy got a phone call from a client who had been dealing with numerous subcontractors. He said Original Copy was the only one that truly had customer service; all the other vendors seemed to give the reasons why they couldn't get something done, while Original found a way to do it. Original Copy had gotten a good-sized job out for him over the weekend, and the customer-service rep was right there and took care of everything. He said Original was a "very service-oriented company."

Nancy attributes this quality to teamwork. "We do not currently have any commissioned salespeople, because we feel the selling end, or the customer service end, is just a piece of the whole pie," she says. "No piece here is more important than the other. I think when you have commission sales, you start finding that salespeople don't necessarily sell for the good of all concerned, which is our company philosophy."

When I ask Nancy if she thought Bright Side had made a difference in salespersons, she says, "Yes, definitely. I think they are looking out more for the good of the customer. They aren't just going to push through a sale. It sounds like the reverse of what a company should look for, but because they're not pushing to make their commission dollars, they're not going to promise something that really can't be done. They instead truly look at things and ask what they can do to help this person out, so we can keep the customer.

"They can't sell anything without the cooperation of everyone in production, marketing, and on and on and on. Before, there was always an attitude that the sales area was the most important and the most prestigious. But if you don't have everyone oriented to the same goal, they can sell until they're blue in the face, and it'll get harder and tougher for sales eventually. I think in a lot of companies, sales is the part that doesn't buy into the team concept."

Instead of commission, Original works on an incentive plan. Instead of dollar volume, unit volume is targeted, so the whole company can get into the fun of achieving goals. The common goal is how many units they can put out in a month; that means sales has to sell it, others have to produce it, the billing department has to bill it.

A caring attitude is important at Original. Nancy says, "It has to come from the person on the top. I have never had a belief that anyone is more important than anyone else. Just like myself. I have a job here, and my job is to be the keeper of the culture: I have to make sure my management focuses on the positive and not on the negative. In every other company I've ever worked in, the people who get all the attention are the negative people. They're the ones who create all the problems. My job is to minimize everything that has to do with those negative people. I think they should just be ignored. If I have thirty people over here who are breaking their necks and trying to get things done, why am I so concerned about the one over there who won't pay attention to the rules, or is tardy all the time? I should spend my whole day on the people who are good.

"Companies are so unfair to the good people! They tend to be forgotten. Your code of conduct, procedure manual, or anything else is only written for the negative, not the positive one. You do have to have some regulations to protect the company so those negative people don't take advantage of it. But then, you should make sure that everything else you do, including benefits, is all oriented to the good people," she says. "That's why we put in an attendance bonus program. When I put in an attendance bonus, I knew who was going to get the money. It was going to be the good people who showed up every day. The negative ones who are giving us a problem don't get the bonus."

To get a bonus, an employee has to have perfect attendance for one quarter, only sixty working days. The quarter division gives more opportunities for success; so if someone gets the flu and loses the bonus for a quarter, he or she has three other chances. The bonus is either one hundred dollars or a day off with pay. A lot of the managers, from a money standpoint, should be taking the day off with pay, but they opt to take the one hundred dollars because they don't want to miss a day. "It gives me an opportunity to reward them for perfect attendance," says Nancy.

Other ways to reward positive behavior include encouraging the positive people and not taking advantage of them by giving them the difficult jobs all the time. While challenging jobs can be a reward for some personalities, Nancy says you have to let them know that you are giving them that job because they are good. "Then they feel really great about it. You can't let them ever get the feeling that you're too busy for them and they just get everything thrown at them," she says.

I remark that there is a lot of negativity out in our culture, a lot of defensive behavior. I ask her how an organization can begin to move in a more positive direction.

"That's a hard one," Nancy responds. "Life philosophies came somewhat naturally to me because of my personality. I'm not greedy. There is a level that I need in order to make my own life nice, but I don't believe in excess. I don't need a lot of stuff. I have a job here like they have a job here. They buy into working for me by realizing that I do share it all, and that I put things back into the company to create more jobs and a solid company that is not on the verge of going bankrupt or laying people off. There is no skimming off the top.

"I went nine years without a paycheck. That's what happens a lot of times in the struggle of making a business work. By the time you finally do experience making any money, you get out of proportion with it. I think I was fortunate enough that I caught myself. I needed a nice car and I got a nice car, but I only needed one. I have a gold watch, but I don't need two of those either. I don't have a fancy life. Everyone here knows how I am. They don't begrudge me. In other places employees always look at their employer, asking, 'Why does he make all of that money? He doesn't do anything! I'm the one who's doing all the work; I'm the one who's sitting here working all the overtime, and he's just going out and living a lavish life.'"

Nancy's employees also know she enjoys coming to work. "I think that's a real strange phenomenon to a lot of them, that I go around and preach how exciting it is. I think we are very privileged that we have great jobs. I would never want to be anywhere else."

A positive attitude toward employees also contributes to a positive environment. No one stands over them with a whip setting all kinds of unrealistic performance standards. Nancy says, "I think everyone wants to achieve. You just give people the opportunity and you set it in front of them, and you trust them to do it. They'll give you a much better job than if you badgered them into it. The one thing I tell everyone who is hired here is: I'll provide the environment; you provide the work. Don't ever think for a second that I don't expect you to hold up your end. Don't think that you are going to come in here and it will be a piece of cake. My standards are very, very high as far as work. So you're going to have to work if you come here. But if you're putting out the work everything else falls into place."

She doesn't tolerate complaining. "If you get a couple of negative people, it seems so easy for them to pull everyone down with them. It can start as simple as, 'Oh I'm so tired today, I don't feel like coming to work. Oh, I wish I didn't have to work; I can't wait until I go home.' Then all of a sudden somebody else is complaining. I tell people I'm not going to put up with it. I worked too darn hard to get this business off the ground. I'm not saying people can't have a down day here and there, but if you have too many of them, you don't deserve the job."

Nancy is willing to help, however. The night before our interview, she called a young man who is usually very positive but all of a sudden was behaving negatively. Nancy called him and asked if there was something wrong. It turned out he was short of money, was trying to accomplish all kinds of things around the holidays, didn't have a car, and didn't want to tell anybody. "To him this was a huge, mammoth problem," Nancy says. "Well, we ended giving him an advance on his pay, and he's back to the positive way he was. I don't want to become a bank for all of my employees, but what is the big deal? This kid has done a heck of a nice job for us for a long time. He had a little problem, so we settled it. We've done this same thing before. We focus on people. Our managers have to be close with their people. They don't have to socialize outside the building, but they have to have a comfortable relationship with that person. And that person also has to be comfortable with me."

I ask Nancy to trace her positive values back to their origin. She credits her childhood but says what changed her life came later. "I was married and had four children; it was a very, very stormy marriage. When I finally got enough nerve to end the marriage, it ended very explosively. He destroyed all the furniture and ripped up all of our clothes and burned them in a big bonfire in the backyard. He did that when I had left one morning to go to my brother's wedding. I discovered it that night when I came home with my four children. I went from having a place to live, clothes, and a pretty decent lifestyle, to having absolutely nothing by the end of that day. Out of seven or eight rooms, a clothes hamper was the only thing that he had not destroyed. He had taken an axe to the refrigerator and the stove, and he told the insurance company that he had done it, so the insurance company covered nothing.

"I remember sitting there and wondering what I was going to do. Unknown to me, my neighbors had heard him and seen him destroying things for over ten hours and had not wanted to get involved. He had been throwing all the winter clothes and stuff out of the attic window onto the fire. The fire department had come and warned him not to have bonfires. I can remember sitting there on the clothes hamper, and my children were in shock. And my kids were young— my youngest daughter was only one. That night I ended up staying with my mother. But she lived in a one-bedroom apartment.

"At one time I thought that was the biggest disaster that happened in my life, but looking back, I see tremendous strength came out of that. No one would rent to me because I was divorced, and of course I had no furniture or money for a deposit. I was working, but my job didn't provide enough money to get myself on my feet, let alone buy bare essentials. I went to welfare and was totally turned off. They said I could have, say, sixty dollars for clothes for my children, and I thought, *You've got to be kidding. I'll do it myself.* We lived with the picnic cooler as our refrigerator for almost a year. I would stop on the way home with ice and milk, and that's how we lived. It was amazing to me that my children never had any concept that having the lights or gas shut off was abnormal. They would call me at work and say, *The lights are out again.* And I said, *Okay, I'll take care of it.* It was not a big deal. And I never overplayed it. They judge you by how you overcome your problems.

"We knew what our goal was. Our goal was to make our lives better. We took one thing at a time. I went out and got three jobs, and my oldest son did the best he could to take care of the smaller kids."

The experience taught Nancy a lot about people and phoniness. "A lot of people think that the whole key is having money, but money really has so little to do with it," Nancy says. "I know so many miserable people with money. The majority of the people who I worked for were miserable people.

"Things did get easier as we got more, and as we made more money, and as my positions changed within companies. That was about a nine- or ten-year span. By the time I decided to open up a company, I had a good credit rating, a very good job, and I was earning decent money."

Opening her own business was similar to what she'd just been through. "I laid everything back on the line again and thought, *Okay I'm going to take a chance to go into something bigger, and if I pull this off I will do it differently from others,*" she says. The difference lies in how she defines a good businessperson: someone who is fair. She says, "In reality I don't have good business skills. I have good people skills. I am a fair person. I have never done anything unethical. However, I will never let anyone walk on me. There is a fine line."

Nancy contrasts her view with what society considers a good businessperson: someone who will cut a deal and step on whomever in order to make money. "I have had some males say to me, 'You will never be successful in business with your attitude.' They view it as a weakness that I am so concerned about the people who work for me." Nancy says she believes the old adage, "You catch more flies with sugar than with vinegar." She says, "I bet 95 percent of my people are as concerned about our customers as I am about them."

Nancy doesn't look for a set profile when hiring people. They acquire her positive philosophy after being in the Original Copy environment. Two out of four welfare recipients she hired have been successful in the company. Most of her managers have progressed through hard work, not "book knowledge." She herself doesn't have a college education. In her words, "We learn what we need to know when we need to know it."

Nancy comments on how she's treated as a woman in the business world. "When I started the business, and I was in charge of the sales, I found it was easier to get a job from a male rather than a female, which was totally the reverse of how I thought it would be. I thought I had a 99 percent chance of getting the job from a woman because she would lean a little bit toward me, but I found instead that if you were close to bankruptcy, well, they might throw you some scraps, but they won't give you a job. We're not nice to our own sex." As for men, Nancy says, "Normally in my business relationships, they just want the job done. It's hard to get them to give you the first opportunity, but then it's up to you. Show them that you can do the job and they don't change in midstream."

Thinking of help for companies who want to change, I ask Nancy how she would change a negative environment in a company. In a small company, she would have private meetings with each person and start weeding through the people to see who would buy into her "culture." She would be more concerned about getting to know the people than getting to know the product, because the people already have been making the product. She would instill in them some of her ideals and values, not asking them to believe the ideals right away, but requiring an open mind to her philosophy because of the changes it would bring. If it were a large company, she would break it down into smaller units, having a person who buys into her philosophy in charge of each group of 100 or 150 people.

The bottom line to eradicating the negative consensus, according to Nancy, is to "sit right out in the middle of it. Get involved or else it's going to be 95 percent negative instead of 95 percent positive. Be right out on that production floor or right in the middle of the accounting department. Don't sit in an office. Be out there, getting to know people; be involved in their everyday working and living."

Throughout Original Copy there is evidence of Nancy's positive ideals. One example is the fostering of employee ideas, even including a beauty seminar. One employee had been a beauty consultant at Estee Lauder. Nancy says, "She said she noticed that some of the women here needed help with their makeup and their hairstyles, and she wondered if she could hold a class. I think she thought that

I would get the marketing people and set everything up. But I told her, 'Since you know how to do this, these are the departments that you will have to utilize. If you can pull it off, here's the budget I can give you. You can put me down as one of the attendees, and just let me know how you're doing.'

"In two months, out of seventy women we have here, about forty-five or fifty showed up after work for a beauty seminar. She expanded upon it. She contacted different distributors and got little gifts to give away, and she made personal gifts for door prizes. Then she wrote a book. She had our design department put it together, and production put it into a really nice format for her. Marketing put a notice in the newsletter and on the bulletin boards, but all at her direction. She also had to do her job during this time. It was really a nice event.

"We had another girl who put together a road rally. Again, I told her basically the same thing. She could advertise it in the newsletter and on the bulletin boards. We would give away T-shirts. But we weren't going to be responsible when people were driving in cars. We didn't want it to be an Original Copy Center event. It was her event. So she would put it together, and we would give some help with the fliers and the printing. So frequently, someone will come up with an idea, and they want to give me the idea and put me in charge of it. That's not what I'm looking for."

Not every idea is acted upon, but Nancy documents each one and invites the appropriate department head to look at it. She respects the ideas.

The annual Halloween party is another example of Nancy's style. She appreciates employees' creativity. "A group of five of our people got together and came as black and white copies—11 x 17 copies. It was really neat because they thought about our product. Some-one else came as a toothbrush using one of our paper boxes. They made bristles coming out of the top. Then they dressed in a sheet of yellow felt that went up over the box. It was a great outfit."

Nancy says the Christmas party is normally a black-tie event. "We also place poinsettias all over and everybody takes them home after-wards. The family picnic in the summer is a lot more casual. We also have a day at Cedar Point amusement park, where we all take the bus out together."

They have anniversary celebrations, Friends and Family Hot Dog Day, and potlucks, too. According to Nancy, "The potlucks are great. For the last one, we invited everyone to bring their favorite dish. We set up tables on the second floor, but we had so many people bring in so much food we had to move into the basement because we didn't have enough room! From that idea, one of the women is doing an Original Copy cookbook of recipes from our own people."

Nancy takes care of the heart and spirit of people so that she has a high-quality company with high-quality service. In closing, I tell her my perspective of her work: I tell her that garbage stuff that other companies are doing out there is Goliath. And what she's doing is David.

"True," she replies. "Although you better make it Nancy, not David. Goliath has been in existence a lot longer, so he's bigger. He's everywhere. But does that mean that we shouldn't try it our way?"

13

Managing Your Bright Side

An Interview with James Krimmel,
President of Zaclon, Inc.

By 1987, Jim Krimmel had worked as an industrial engineer for more than a decade and a half. But as his employer, DuPont, considered closing the ancient Cleveland plant where he worked—a plant that had been in operation for well over a century—he and a partner, Joe Turgeon, put together financing and a plan for purchasing the plant and operating it independently.

In becoming a part-owner, he has had the opportunity to put into practice some of his still-emerging ideas about participative management—or as he calls it, "business without managers"—that he shares with other companies as a leader in the Ohio Manufacturers' Association.

While losing the safety net provided by a Fortune 500 company caused nervousness at first, his company, Zaclon, remains the world's largest producer of zinc ammonium chloride, which is used as a coating in the galvanizing process by producers of pipeline, guardrail, and other galvanized-steel products. Zaclon supplies about three-

92

quarters of the U.S. market for galvanizing fluxes and about 35 percent of the worldwide total.

In this chapter, the forty-seven-year-old Krimmel discusses the transition from traditional large-company ownership and management to a smaller, more entrepreneurial group that not only encourages but also expects every employee to reach his or her potential.

I ask what would have happened to the plant had Krimmel and his partner not bought it. Jim says, "It would have been shut down. And DuPont was concerned about that, which is why they preferred to sell to us. DuPont had tried to sell it about three years prior to our purchase, but they couldn't find any serious buyers. It was losing money for them." The Cleveland plant produced stable products, but DuPont was interested in growth products. The plant was small-volume and required more marketing attention than it was getting. The plant was also old—DuPont hadn't invested in it in ten years.

One reason DuPont preferred to sell than to close is because, as Jim says, "Shutting down a chemical plant is not very cheap today. They knew that there would be probably about a $25-million cleanup liability if they shut it down. It's been in operation since 1866, and there weren't too many environmental regulations in place at that time. In fact, in 1966 there weren't very many. It wasn't until the '70s really that most of that came."

The transition wasn't easy. "It was very traumatic for all of us to not have DuPont anymore," Jim says. "DuPont was lifetime employment. We felt confident they'd take care of us. I remember a nightmare I had one of the first days after we took over. I saw myself having my skin ripped from my body. It felt so real I woke up in the middle of the night. It was from fear for all the little things you don't think about, like setting up phone systems, that are the entitlements of working for a large company. Suddenly, they aren't there any more, and you have to decide what to do."

Krimmel's decisions included a vision for his new company. "From the beginning," he says, "I had a mental model, because the concept of trying to engage the entire workforce was being discussed in management circles at the time. Eventually, I tried to put a model on paper that showed interlocking teams working together to accomplish things with, essentially, no line supervision. That's the key, really, and it's not comfortable for hourly people or for salaried people. It's very comfortable to have line managers who theoretically have responsibility for everything. Both from the top—you can go to them and beat on them—and from the bottom—they can delegate everything. And that poor guy in the middle wasn't really in control, except on paper."

Part of Krimmel's objective in moving into a businesses-without-managers philosophy and fully engaging the workforce is so that the workforce can handle not only routine labor but also the concepts of incremental improvement. The workers do the things they can do best, because they know those things better than management. Then the lesser, more skeletal resource organization handles the quantum leaps and major-step improvements.

Jim incorporated his changes gradually, allowing time to get systems in place and customer bases realigned. "Then we started focusing on what we really wanted to be as a company. We developed a vision statement. When I thought about how to get from where I was to where I wanted to be, what came to me is to just eliminate the structure that supported the more traditional organization. I recognized that we'd have some problems, but I thought we should do it anyhow. So today there's no longer any line supervision by management," he says.

I ask him what it was like to suddenly stop relying on that middle-management buffer between managers and line employees. He answers, "It's very unsettling at both ends to not have that. Managers have to work directly with the people doing the work. People on the floor have to take responsibility for conflict resolution and everything else. And that's the toughest part of the whole thing. It's not someone else's responsibility anymore—it's all of our responsibilities. At first, production people would come to me and say, 'What do I do?' or 'How do I do this?' And I would say, 'I don't know how you do that or what you should do. What do you think? What are we trying to accomplish?'"

While Jim took a lot of humanities, psychology, sociology, and management theory courses in college, "None of it prepared me for the real world and what it's really all about. What drove me to looking for a better way is that for twenty years, I tried the traditional way. And I know it doesn't work. I don't know if this way works or not, but I think it does. And I think that it's got a much better chance of succeeding than some of the more traditional bureaucratic, autocratic, hierarchical structures. It's really letting people use their full capabilities to the benefit of the business, and having a little fun besides. But even with this system, you've got to keep at it. It's easy to get lazy and forget that this takes constant work and attention and repair and restrategizing and everything else. It's easy to sugar-coat what's really going on in any company. There's still conflict, there's still development, there's still resistance. But it's waning. And I think people see the benefit to them individually.

"The biggest barrier to the open style of management is the fact that some people consider certain coworkers as being incapable of functioning in that more egalitarian environment where everyone takes personal responsibility for his or her own job," Krimmel says. "But I think everyone is fully capable of functioning in that environment; they just don't realize it themselves sometimes. I try to get some of our managers to take a risk and give people a little more responsibility when they are not really confident that they are able to handle it. Part of our culture, Zaclon culture, is we expect people to take risks. When you take risks, you are going to fall occasionally, but if you give people that responsibility and show them you believe they can do it, in time they will. I think that is a very powerful tool."

As Jim hired his original workforce, DuPont gave him the time and place to interview every DuPont employee who worked at the site. "I talked to them about the way we planned to operate, including becoming more responsible for self, not understanding at the time we would go as quickly or as far as we did. I worked with all these people for twenty years, and I tried not to let my prejudices decide who I would offer a job to. I made formal job offers to people; most accepted. We went from ninety or ninety-five people under DuPont to fifty or so. And we laid out very clearly that there was going to be a wage-rate reduction of two dollars an hour; that we were going to offer a profit-sharing plan, which we offered from day one; and that we would expect them to think more than they were required to do under DuPont. People are very well paid here. Our hourly employees earn wages that rival a major manufacturing company. We intentionally understaffed by 20 percent and made it up on overtime. Even when we cut everyone's hourly rate two dollars an hour, they were still earning more than they were before."

While Krimmel doesn't often have to fill new positions—Zaclon's turnover rate is only two people a year—his hiring process is special. If there is a vacancy in the production area, the process starts by having the production people interview candidates. Krimmel says, "The candidates are generated by traditional means, such as newspaper ads, but first we encourage people to bring friends. We think that's a good way to get good people. You don't recommend someone to work with you if you don't think rather highly of them. The production teams look at the responses, pick the ones they want to talk to, and they conduct a series of interviews and take it down to a top two or three list. I tend to talk to them only when it's down to one or two people, just to make sure that I'm fairly comfortable with the selection of the team. But they basically select who they're going to hire. That way, you're almost assured of success, because a team of people will help this person along. They don't want to look like they made the wrong decision, for one thing. So they work more closely with them." The new person is not someone imposed on employees by management.

While most of the workforce handles routine labor and incremental improvements, Jim's resource organization strives for the "quantum leaps" he envisions. As he explains, "We have a new-business development team that spends 20 percent of their time exploring new business opportunities unrelated to our current business. We do a lot of pure research, not all of it focused on our existing business in galvanizing products. For instance, we're working on methods for controlling zebra mussels, and we're working on road surface materials. They research anything that's related to chemistry, and we're starting to think about some things that aren't related to chemistry." He receives about forty magazines, his favorite being a NASA tech book, full of everything NASA scientists are working on. "I'm always looking to see if there's something there for us."

Krimmel says he receives mixed reactions to his management philosophies from other manufacturers. "I get everything from people nodding their head and saying, 'Gee—that's interesting. How do you do this?' to people shaking their heads and saying, 'That would never work for us because . . .' Whether it will work or not for them is not my concern. I share with my counterparts where I can. I do have a mission in life, which is to help improve the productivity of U.S. manufacturers. This sharing of information with other owners and managers about our management style is one of the vehicles that allows me to do that. But I try to sell it more on a soft-sell basis than a hard-sell basis. It's a difficult leap for a lot of people. And yet, how can anyone not believe that the right way is to engage the workforce? I don't think anyone could disagree. How could anyone disagree that fully utilizing the capabilities of every person working for you will improve the process? How can there be an argument?"

What lies ahead for Krimmel? He says, "Right now, I'm learning for my next career, which will be helping other companies embrace this style of management and become more productive as a result." He's not sure when this next career will be, maybe in five or ten years, but he's increasingly getting more involved outside of the company.

What lies ahead for Zaclon? Krimmel says, "Once you have a vision of where you're going, you just start moving and see where you end up. The process of discovery is really what it's all about. If you really trust people, and you trust the abilities of people, you let them take you where it's logical to go. You just do it."

Part 4

Play with Bright Side Tools

One day I made a quick stop at a Federal Express office. Another woman in line had a box containing a teddy bear and medicine. The toy and medicine were for a four-year-old child in Florida with cancer. The woman told me that she gave away bears, baseball caps, and trips to Disney World to cancer patients.

"What age kids?" I inquired.

Smiling, but without pausing, she responded, "All age kids. Aren't we always children?"

She was right, of course. But the sad truth is that it's easy to drift away from our inner youthfulness as we age. In order to recapture the exuberant sense of discovery of youth and to shatter the strictures of routine and habit, in my workshops I use a number of simple, creativity-building methods, which are described in the following section. You'll learn about how simple items such as crayons, stickers, and balloons can spark our imaginations and reconnect us to childhood, a time when we honored possibilities more than limits. As the diagram shows, when we learn to build trust, truth, and belief in ourselves, we begin a momentum for learning.

As you read through these exercises and the examples of how various organizations have applied them, I hope you'll consider applying the lessons to your own life and your specific circumstances. You might ask yourself the following questions: What did I experience? What was my internal dialogue as I read about these? And then, as you consider your own problems and challenges, What specific action steps might I take? The final part of this book provides exercises to help you apply these lessons.

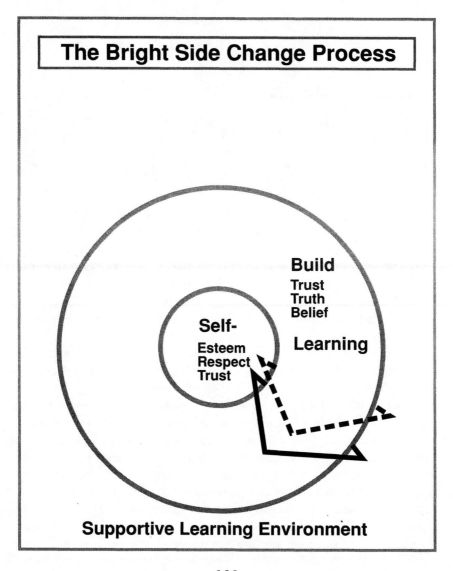

The Bright Side Change Process

Build
Trust
Truth
Belief

Self-
Esteem
Respect
Trust

Learning

Supportive Learning Environment

How wonderful it is being five years old. At that age, we know how to have fun, we know how to play. And creativity isn't reserved for the genius, but we are each highly creative in our own individual areas of genius.

Every human being is a talented individual filled with genius and a child's wonderful enthusiasm. The American challenge is to free that child and to rediscover individual giftedness and national greatness.

That precious kindergartner that lives within gets squashed as we grow up. Growing taller, bigger, and stronger suffocates the optimism, joy, and gentleness that is so abundant when we are five. The simplest way to release your kindergartner is to pull out a childhood toy of joy. In these next chapters, I will try to give you tools for releasing your creative five-year-old and your childlike potential.

14

Tools of Wonder

It was Christmas. My daughter and I went to get our Christmas tree. As we browsed and searched, none of the trees measured up to our expectations of the perfect tree. Dismayed, I wondered if this would be the Christmas without the magic of discovering the tree just for us.

A helpful man suggested we cut down our own tree. Ordinarily, I would immediately dismiss that kind of suggestion. After all, I had never sawed anything, let alone held a saw in my hands. I chuckled to myself, remembering how shocked my son was when I sewed a button on his shirt. He exclaimed, "Mom, you can sew!"

But a Christmas without magic is like no Christmas at all. So I made a decision. "I will cut the tree down," I announced.

Off we trudged through acres of beautiful pines, searching out the perfect one. Then we saw it, big and majestic against the bright blue sky. Satisfied, I turned my attention to the task. I began to think negative thoughts.

I'm never going to be able to do this, I thought.

But aloud I said, "Well, let's get going."

How am I going to do this? I worried to myself. To my daughter I said, "Well, I better lie on the ground to get the right angle" (as if I knew).

This is awful, I thought to myself. *I am simply going to pretend I know what I am doing.*

With each anguished thought, I could hear my daughter encourage me with "That's great, Mom." I knew I couldn't disappoint her or myself. I decided that even if it took me hours and hours, I would cut that tree down!

I began to saw. Nothing happened. The saw got stuck. My daughter continued to encourage me, saying that she was pulling the tree toward her to give it a little help. *Good,* I thought. *She hasn't caught on to how inadequate I feel.* I was struck by the hope, excitement, and pure confidence in her voice that said, "Yes, Mom, you can do it!"

Don't give up, I told myself. *Keep trying.* With that, I made my first cut. *Maybe I can saw down a tree after all,* I inwardly rejoiced.

Maressa pulled harder. I worked faster. With each cut I repeated, *Yes, I can; I am doing it,* until Maressa loudly, jubilantly bellowed, "Tim-berrr!"

We celebrated, dancing, laughing, and hugging. We did it! It was wonderful.

It was empowering to shatter a concept of self that had been painted by our culture and my family regarding the roles for women and men. What limiting beliefs do we need to shatter to help ourselves unlock hidden talents, use more of our resources, and realize more of our dreams? How can you access your childhood characteristics of optimism, vitality, and creativity?

The tools we need to access them are toys of wonder. I am always amazed and moved when I see Bright Side participants move from resistance, fear, and skepticism to exuberance, creativity, openness, and trust by using the Bright Side tools and techniques. A transformation occurs once participants begin to experience positive energy and emotion.

When I first saw people respond to the process, I knew something powerful and special was happening. When I saw the same response in all ages, both sexes, and all socioeconomic backgrounds, I knew the ideas that I had developed for self-realization and empowerment were universal. What I have also seen is that most of us, to some degree, come from family and cultural roles that have wounded us.

The Bright Side tools work. They build a simple, easily remembered, positive image. They are concrete and can be used daily to break out of old negative behavior patterns and to get us thinking in new ways. The tools are energizing and renewing because they bring uplifting pictures to mind. They remind us that we create our own moods and states of motivation. They also activate positive memories from the past. The tools slap our senses like cold water being splashed on our body, breaking stress and tension. They stimulate and improve our brain function.

As psychologist Abraham Maslow said, "If the only tool you have is a hammer, you tend to see every problem as a nail." Maslow believed that psychology dealt too much with human frailty and not enough with human strength. He looked to a more positive side of humanity. To garden our spirits and to nurture the child within, we need the tools of childhood—the toys of wonder.

Crayons

Even the smell of crayons will bring back memories and feelings of your magical early years. Crayons break the habit of black and white. They are a colorful reminder that we can shatter limiting beliefs and paint visions of a new self, a new organization, or a new product.

One executive I know keeps crayons on her desk to doodle new ideas and concepts. A group of managers joined a work team member in order to discuss their differences and a life event that shaped them into who they are today. They discovered more similarities than differences. Then they drew large pictures of each other as they each imagined the other to be as a young child. In a very playful manner, they built trust by risking their own thoughts and by learning more about each other.

Red Balls and Jacks

This childhood toy helps us recall our own "Red Ball Jets" past positive experience. The jacks symbolize letting go of the negative and filling with the positive. The red ball itself carries the picture of this positive experience. The red ball reminds us to be resilient and to bounce back. This familiar children's game is one of the best exercises for the cerebellum. It requires hand speed and coordination. Exercise increases mood and brain functioning—we think better and feel better. It is also a reminder that repetition creates change in our brain cells. Practice helps us learn and change.

Bubbles

This is a "solution" that washes away years of fear and mistrust. It cleanses the mind, heart, and spirit to reveal childhood spontaneity and purity. It is a symbol for the childhood language of love, freedom, and truth. It is for bubbling our creative wonder and individuality. It is the single most important tool for personal empowerment.

Because some people are uncomfortable with the idea of toys at work, I once experimented with the paddles and balls that are attached by rubber bands, thinking those toys would be more masculine and acceptable than bubbles. Those paddles and balls brought back memories of how difficult it is to use that toy. Most participants wanted to trade them in for soap bubbles or balls and jacks. Often the toy-of-choice is the bubbles. Simple. Splendid. Creative. Pure. Joyful. Bubbles.

So grab your bubbles and begin to activate your positive child self. Recall the games you played with bubbles as a child. Picture yourself blowing hundreds of bubbles or an absolutely huge bubble. As you bubble, recall more of the childhood joy of simplicity. Feel the oxygen cleanse your body with each bubble-blowing breath. Breathe in goodness and breathe out tension.

Allow yourself to become more imaginative. What are the different ways you can blow bubbles? Can you develop a new way to blow bubbles? Can you blow a bubble inside a bubble? How about a bubble chain? Can you put your finger inside the bubble without breaking it? (Be sure your finger is thoroughly covered with bubble soap before inserting it!) Incidentally, if you answered no to any of these questions, you need to play more in order to relax your mind and activate the right side of your brain.

Bubbling relaxes the mind and body. Relaxation is necessary for peak performance and health. It reconnects us to that tender, lovable, positive child that lives within us.

Let your tender child come out. Picture yourself at age five blowing bubbles.

As you continue bubbling, begin to put positive emotions, ideas, and thoughts in those bubbles. Visualize your dreams and goals. Place those pictures of success in the bubble. If a negative idea catapults from your mind, stomp or break the bubble that is holding that idea. Begin to put feelings of love for others inside your bubbles. Express feelings of forgiveness for yourself and others in order to let go of barriers that hinder you or your success.

Blowing bubbles certainly beats arguing, according to one Bright Side participant. She keeps her bubbles out on the kitchen counter. Frequently, when things are tense in their household, the family blows bubbles to break the tension. "It's better than blowing hot air and regretting angry words," she explains.

One group of employees uses the office fan to blow bubbles every Friday afternoon. It's a simple way to revitalize the team, get more energized at the end of the week, and to recall the positive experience of the Bright Side workshop.

One of Bright Side's associates went out on a sunny afternoon with three friends and two bottles of bubbles. Needless to say, blowing bubbles in town brought laughter, both to them and to bystanders. One man tried the Bright Side suggestion of blowing bubbles in different ways. He walked backwards while trying to blow bubbles. Try as he did, he simply could not coordinate those two efforts. Recently, in a job interview, when asked about anything he couldn't do, he quickly remarked, "I can't walk backwards and blow bubbles at the same time." His skillful sense of humor broke the barrier of formality and endeared him to the prospective employer. He got the job. (No doubt he was bubbling positive images of success!)

The most touching example I have about bubbling comes from a mother who told me about her child's bubble experience. As a gift to my son and daughter, I present Bright Side programs to their school classes. A full year following one of my school presentations, a mother came up to me to tell me that her daughter begins each morning by bubble blowing, filling those bubbles with positive affirmations about being lovable and awesome. Try it. Blow those bubbles and place inside each one loving, encouraging, affirming statements about your very own awesomeness.

"Awesome" Stickers

These remind us that we are worthy and awesome. They remind us to start each day fresh with the awesome cheer:

I am awesome
You are awesome
We are awesome
Yes! Yes! Yes!

The "Awesome" stickers remind us of the vital importance of positive self-talk, belief in self, and encouraging feedback. The cheer is a simple way to build energy and vitality. The following story is an example of how it brings out the champion self.

It was my son's championship basketball game in the fourth grade. It was his first season playing basketball, and he was thrilled with the prospect of being on a championship team. It was the first time *his* team in any sport had made it to the finals.

I had "Awesome" stickers from Bright Side workshops and wondered about taking those stickers to the players and coach. Knowing how kids sometimes feel about what their parents do, I cautiously but optimistically asked my nine-year-old what he thought about the sticker idea. As it turned out, he thought it was an awesome idea!

The coach thought it was an awesome idea, too. He placed the stickers on himself and on all four assistant coaches. Then, he went to each player and placed an "Awesome" sticker on his sleeve, giving each individual a pat on the back and positive words of encouragement. The boys smiled. Their faces actually glowed. They became noticeably more relaxed, and I heard them calling each other awesome. And awesome they were! They won the championship game, against a team they had never beaten, by more than ten points! Never underestimate the power of awesome thinking and the awesome cheer.

Stars

The one novel Bright Side tool that is almost universally popular is a star. When is the last time that you received a star? If you are like most Bright Side participants, you will say that it was in kindergarten or grade school.

Recalling that experience, you can surely feel your spirits soar. Then why has it been so many years since you have received that symbol of goodwill?

The stars, because they relate to our innocent, playful, positive self, activate the healthy memories within us. It is always exciting to see how exuberantly people respond when they discover that they will be receiving a packet of gold stars. The reaction is universal and felt by employees in all professional categories.

Stars are used to help trigger early memories of goodness, value, and worth; to remind us of the powerful importance of meeting psychological needs; to hold others in positive regard; to find something to respect and care for in all people—especially ourselves; and to give lots of positive feedback.

Motivation is controlled by our mood state. The mood state we are in influences the mood state of those around us. After seeing the exuberant responses of Bright Side participants while giving or receiving positive feedback coupled with using the stars, I am convinced that the cornerstone to an enhanced motivation state is verbalized positive regard for self and others.

"What's Important Is You" Postcard

In workshops, we'll often encourage participants to write out commitments to personal action on a postcard. We'll collect these and mail them back to people as personal reminders. Or a participant can choose to write encouragements to a learning partner and later mail that postcard to her as a reinforcement. We might develop proverbs, such as Goethe's familiar quote: "Treat a man as he is and he will remain as he is. Treat a person as he can and should be and he will become as he can and should be." Or perhaps we'll have participants quote one another on postcards, post-it notes, or in learning journals. These "what's important is you" postcards serve as a tangible reinforcement to learning.

Red Ball Stickers

These stickers are strategically placed on telephones, mirrors, car dashboards, and briefcases to visually remind us to recall and use our energized past positive, our own "Red Ball Jets" experience. Participants are encouraged to practice daily bringing this past positive state of mind and to use a past positive nickname whenever feeling tense, anxious, or uncertain. This image is strengthened through meditation and visualization.

Flashlights

A symbol of shedding light and awareness, flashlights can be used to represent the illumination of new choices. They can serve as tools to brighten our dark side.

Book Bags

Stenciled with exhortations to learning or other cheerful messages, they can signify the notion that we need to employ an assortment of tools to assist in creating change.

Balloons

Balloons represent celebration, festivities, and success. Balloons bring back childhood memories of play. They can be used in a variety of toss games:

- Keep the balloon in the air.
- Keep several balloons in the air.
- Use only your head (or any other part of your body) to keep the balloon afloat.

Team members can join up with a partner, back-to-back, each with a balloon in hand, and create a playful (maybe outrageous) use of the balloon with his or her partner. Team members can blow up a balloon, filling it with negative, limiting, or critical thoughts, ideas, and feelings. Once the balloons are blown up, all team members let go of the balloons, thus letting go of the negatives. Similarly, team members can blow up a balloon, filling it with the negative. Once blown up, the balloon is tied. The negative is stomped out of the balloon.

Gray Matter

We stretch, shape, and form clay as we generate more ideas, release ideas, and discover new solutions. I ask participants individually to come up with as many different uses, titles, and names for the gray matter as they can in a three-minute period. They are asked to count the number of ideas when finished.

Participants either freeze or relax during this exercise. Those who freeze and become overly serious generate between three and five ideas. Those who relax and become playful come up with ten to twenty.

I then ask participants to form groups of six to eight people. First, they are to collectively count their total number of ideas. This total generally ranges from eighteen to thirty. They are then given another three minutes to generate another twenty-five to thirty brand-new uses or titles. Participants are usually apprehensive, wondering how they can possibly generate even more ideas.

But this attempt is a team effort. The teams are usually successful, sometimes producing a quantity greater than requested.

When there are four or five teams or more, it is not uncommon for the results of the exercise to exceed one hundred to two hundred fresh ideas, a wonderful surprise to most Bright Side participants. At Zaclon, when the company was financially challenged, Joe Turgeon and Jim Krimmel would recall how easy it was in Bright Side seminars for them to create hundreds of gray-matter uses. They applied that exercise to creating solutions for a new and successful financial strategy.

Many Bright Side participants keep this "gray matter" putty on their desk or in a pocket to serve as a reminder that we can generate hundreds of alternatives or solutions to any of our life challenges.

I recall once watching a six- to nine-month-old child. What curiosity and persistence I observed! This infant had rolled into a lowered area in between cushions and pillows and was experimenting with dozens of ways to move out. Stretching and trying many ideas, without giving up, she finally discovered the solution.

Gray matter also reminds us to play and be as creative as children.

The Bright Side Hug Card

I have noticed that winning teams and winning athletes hug, kiss, and touch. Studies have demonstrated that winners hug and get hugged more often than losers. One study at Ohio State University showed that rabbits remained healthy, in spite of a high-fat diet, as a result of much petting and stroking.

Team spirit and human health are greatly enhanced by various approaches to hugs. In Bright Side seminars, coworkers are encouraged to appropriately hug each other, whether it is a huddle hug, a high-five, or a bear hug. Many of us are uncomfortable with such an open expression of touch because we have learned about touch in the wrong ways. But the cards remind us of the vital importance of hugging, holding, and touching and how they can give life richer, greater meaning. The form the card takes isn't very important, and can vary widely based on the particular goal of the participants. But the idea is the same in every case: to adapt a hug or some other vehicle for building unity into a team's spirit-building ritual. At one company, Timken, workshop participants developed their own cheer:

> The team is in the huddle,
>   we want to get ahead.
> We looked at one another
>   and this is what we said:
> We gotta T-R-I-S-K. Yes! Yes! Yes!

We must take risks (we will learn what *trisk* means in chapter 18) and touch. Hugging is a natural instinct. Touch facilitates trust and empathy. Infants die, and children can become severely depressed when deprived of touch over a period of time.

In *Build Your Brain Power: The Latest Techniques to Preserve, Restore, and Improve Your Brain's Potential*, Arthur Winter, M.D. and Ruth Winter write that the brain can be developed and repaired, to a degree, even in old age; and that we can train the brain to preserve, restore, and improve intellect through selective stimulation. We use between .01 and 10 percent of our brain capacity. Research shows that decline in mental function is not an inevitable part of aging. It is believed that an enriching environment increases the manufacturing of the brain's glial cells, which provide support to the neurons there.

These neurons perform the main work of the brain, processing impulses from far-flung nerves of the sense organs. Thus, the stimulating Bright Side tools of wonder help our brain function and keep us young and vibrant. To obtain your own "Awesome" stickers, or "What's Important Is You" postcards, contact Bright Side at (216) 247-2611.

15

Outrageous!

Successful organizations generally have at least a touch of outrageousness, a restless desire to break out of constraints. These are companies that are successful and prosperous and yet have a heart of both love and fun. They're all about curiosity, celebration, fearlessness, learning, challenges, and fun! It's their spirit of fun that feeds change and inventiveness. Edison possessed it, as did Sam Walton and other great heroes you've read about. As Lester Thurow, dean of the Massachusetts Institute of Technology's School of Management wrote in *Head to Head* (quoting a Buddhist text):

> The Master in the art of living makes little distinction between his work and his play, his labor and his leisure, his mind and his body, his education and his recreation, his love and his religion. He hardly knows which is which. He simply pursues his vision of excellence in whatever he does, leaving others to decide whether he is working or playing. To him he is always doing both.[4]

When he traveled through Japan and Korea in 1975, Sam Walton observed methods used to motivate employees and have fun. Eager to foster creativity by doing wild and outrageous things in his own organization, and always thirsting to find a better way, he borrowed the good ideas he discovered. He hoped to stimulate his people to think of unusual ways to delight Wal-Mart customers.

Fun Ideas

These are some of the ideas he introduced to bring the spirit of fun into his stores, as he described in *Sam Walton, Made in America: My Story.*

Our Fairbury, Nebraska, store has a "precision shopping cart drill team" that marches in local parades. The members all wear Wal-Mart smocks and push their carts through a routine of whirls, twirls, circles, and crossovers. Our Cedartown, Georgia, store holds a kiss-the-pig contest to raise money for charity. They set out jars with each manager's name on them, and the manager whose jar winds up with the most donations has to kiss a pig. Our New Iberia, Louisiana, store fields a cheerleading squad called the Shrinkettes. Their cheers deal with what else? Cutting shrinkage: "WHAT DO YOU DO ABOUT SHRINKAGE? CRUSH IT! CRUSH IT!" The Shrinkettes stole the show at one of our Wal-Mart annual meetings with cheers like: "CALIFORNIA ORANGES, TEXAS CACTUS, WE THINK K-MART COULD USE SOME PRACTICE!" Our Fitzgerald, Georgia, store won first place in the Irwin County Sweet Potato Parade with a float featuring seven associates dressed as fruits and vegetables grown in south Georgia. As they passed the judging stand, the homegrown fruits and vegetables did a homegrown Wal-Mart cheer. Managers from our Ozark, Missouri, store dressed up in pink tutus, got on the back of a flatbed truck, and cruised the town square on Friday night, the peak time for teenage cruisers, and somehow managed to raise money for charity by doing it.[5]

The Wal-Mart cheer, songs, and exercises are unexpectedly incorporated into Wal-Mart meetings. The ultimate purpose of fun is to create spontaneity and spirit, to lighten up. This fun and unpredictability help minimize resistance to change.

Consider these unconventional means by which one company, the IBM data-processing subsidiary Integrated Systems Solutions Corporation (ISSC), consciously attempts to breed a spirit of fun.

The Horse Race. ISSC once held its annual meeting at a local racetrack. Everyone was given play money to bet on horse races that were prerecorded. Then came the surprise: The last race featured the managers! There were three managers to a team, two of whom wore horse costumes, while a third sat on a sulky. With names like Double-Double (for the heaviest team, of course), five teams pranced, galloped, and swayed in ways that redefine how horses move. These teams trudged through muddy soup and a deluge of rain! Amidst the muddy fun a couple of lessons were learned. First, the winning team won because the other four teams were intent on cutting off the fastest competition. Second, as individuals lost their play money in betting, they formed teams to pool what was left for the auction of really great gifts—increasing their odds of winning a gift.

Team Bowling. This meeting saw associates gathered at the local bowling alley dressed in the '50s style: slicked hair, poodle skirts, and T-shirts. Teams had each member bowl a single frame, which was a clever way to build cooperation. For the play-offs, the best and worst teams were paired for bumper bowling. Bumpers were placed along the gutters, and the bowlers had to hit the gutter first, or the frame didn't count. Of course, with this system, the worst bowlers were the best.

Leader of the Pack. The leadership team rock 'n rolled to create an ISSC hit video, "Leader of the Pack." The director of systems delivery, Pete Wilzbach, greased his hair down and looked hip in a black leather jacket topped off with big, heavy chains. He and the ISSC chorus oohed and aahed in scenes shot at a candy store and malt shop. Best yet, Wilzbach rode a little red motorcycle down ISSC hallways and in and out of the ISSC elevator! It's ISSC's way to celebrate.

Rewards

Rewards are also fun at ISSC. One means by which ISSC rewarded its employees was called the Military Operation. This celebration honored eighty ISSC associates who worked around the clock, away from home, to meet a client's October 26 deadline. Everything was a parody of the military operation launched during the Gulf War of the early '90s. The celebration was presented in terms of ground warfare, perfect battle plan, and face-to-face combat. Managers took on the persona of the president or a general. The stage was highlighted with a huge American flag and great hanging stars. The associates' hard work and personal sacrifice was rewarded with $250–$1,500 cash awards totaling more than $30,000.

All employees love being told they are appreciated. And ISSC has one of the most exciting and enjoyable approaches to providing motivating feedback and recognition. It has given away a flashy, red sports car to the individual who determined ways to eliminate defects.

Employees receive Petey Bucks, cleverly named after Wilzbach, as a reward for process efficiency or team effectiveness. The first level of trade for Petey Bucks is breakfast with Wilzbach. This provides an important setting for sharing new ideas. The sports car now goes to the team with the highest average of Petey Bucks. The team members must figure out how to share it. ISSC went from management thanking people to people thanking people.

Another form of recognition at ISSC is "diverdends" (Bob Diver is the new director of ISSC, Lexington). For starters, everyone receives a share of ISSC stock. Then, when a team exceeds targeted profit, that additional profit is equally shared among all associates. However, this is balanced with customer satisfaction. If customer satisfaction is below the ISSC average, there is no bonus. Fun, celebration, and recognition are combined to motivate people and exceed customer expectations. This is one way that ISSC stays in the forefront of change.

For many people, the novel gift of congratulations gives them the praise and recognition to encourage them to continue growing. At Manco, CEO Jack Kahl presented a challenge to his team: If they reached sales of $60 million at the end of the fiscal year, Kahl promised to swim the duck pond in front of Manco's corporate headquarters. The team reached their goal; Kahl kept his word.

The event blossomed into a celebration that featured a high school marching band and a buffet luncheon. The Manco cafeteria was filled with balloons bearing Manco colors. Despite damp, cold weather, the entire company marched out with Kahl on the designated day. He sported several bathing suits, all cleverly made just for this event. The mood and energy were high. He did swim the pond. He followed the memorable endeavor with bonus checks that were individually presented at the luncheon. Documented acknowledgments of hard work were given to each Manco partner. Kahl's novel approach broke out of the boundaries.

His inclusion of a bonus for the team achievement was complemented with a community gift of fifty thousand dollars to Providence House, a crisis nursery in Cleveland. Sister Hope, founder of Providence House, was present. As Manco's leader, he dared to take a risk. The entire day—swim, rewards, lunch—created an environment of exceptional energy and benevolence. Who would not want to work hard again next year?

At one company, employees were asked to create a variety of ways they could make positive contributions to make a difference at the company. Before they went home, they were told that all employees would receive a gift of fun. At a subsequent meeting, a member passed out peanuts in a shell, each with a memo that said, "Sometimes I feel like a nut."

Of course, there are less outrageous ways to reward employees. At Zaclon's annual picnic, president Jim Krimmel and chairman Joe Turgeon grill steaks on the plant grounds for the entire Zaclon team.

The Pledge

Sam Walton asked his people to agree to a pledge that, despite its simplicity, was outrageous at the time for an American manager.

> I don't think any other retail company in the world could do what I'm going to propose to you. It's simple. It won't cost us anything. And I believe it would just work magic, absolute magic on our customers, and our sales would escalate, and I think we'd just shoot past our K-Mart friends in a year or two and probably Sears as well. I want you to take a pledge with me. I want you to promise that whenever you come within ten feet of a customer, you will look him in the eye, greet him, and ask him if you can help him. Now I know some of you are just naturally shy, and maybe don't want to bother folks. But if you'll go along with me on this, it would, I'm sure, help you become a leader. It would help your personality develop, you would become more outgoing, and in time you might become manager of that store, you might

become a department manager, you might become a district manager, or whatever you choose to be in the company. It will do wonders for you. I guarantee it.[6]

This pledge has been the key to Walton's success. And those were no empty words, imploring employees to work harder simply for the benefit of someone else. Into the retail industry, an industry that usually treated people with little respect, Walton consciously wove inducements for his employees to respect customers.

Empowerment

Another outrageous idea of Sam Walton's concerned employee empowerment.

> The larger truth that I failed to see turned out to be another of those paradoxes—like the discounter's principle of the less you charge, the more you'll earn. And here it is: the more you share profits with your associates—whether it's in salaries or incentives or bonuses or stock discounts—the more profit will accrue to the company. Why? Because the way management treats associates is exactly how the associates will then treat the customers. And if the associates treat the customers well, the customer will return again and again, and that is where the real profit in this business lies, not in trying to drag strangers into your stores for one-time purchases based on splashy sales or expensive advertising. Satisfied, loyal, repeat customers are at the heart of Wal-Mart's spectacular profit margins, and those customers are loyal to us because our associates treat them better than salespeople in other stores do. So, in the whole Wal-Mart scheme of things, the most important contact ever made is between the associates in the store and the customer.[7]

Through giving authority from the outset, the empowerment process is not unlike pushing an eaglet from its nest. An eagle's nest rests high on a mountainside. The parent will push the eaglet out of the nest if it has not already left the security of the nest to test its wings. The parent will fly under the young bird to catch it should it fail in its first attempt at flying. Giving authority is similar. By providing caring environments, where management offers the same blend of challenge and support, people can be encouraged to be their best.

As Pete Wilzbach says, "The successful company of the future will be the one where the people are adept at handling rapid change and chaos. Customers are asking businesses to solve problems that have never been solved before, so the premium will be on creativity, empowerment and risk-taking." Perhaps the biggest premium in this new environment, he might have added, will be on gifted, courageous managers such as himself who free their organizations to break out of boxes and reach for the stars.

16

Play Can Be Productive

The tools that have great power today are often those of control and violence. Not only guns and drugs but also corporate mergers and acquisitions are weapons in our society. Just as life can be ruined by a critical injury from a gun, lives are ruined by buying, selling, restructuring, divesting, and merging. These weapons help snuff out the richness of each individual, for the profit of a few.

People have become familiar, and thus quite comfortable, with tools of destruction. It is often deemed appropriate and acceptable for people at home or at work to be verbally defensive and abusive, cursing at each other with belittling remarks or sarcastic humor: "That's a stupid idea"; "That's crazy"; "Your head is so small you must have a tiny brain." The tongue is potentially our most destructive weapon. Working with corporations, I am shocked at how frequently people belittle and nibble away at each other.

Such behavior is so common that we are uncomfortable with the healthy tools of creativity and fun. The defensive, rejecting behavior of corporate America is accepted as normal. We have been socialized and conditioned to use and accept defensive behavior.

In contrast to the destructive tools of aggression, defensiveness, and verbal abuse, play is a productive tool. Play helps us:

121

reduce stress
remember positive childhood experiences
reframe our current perceptions, ideas, or thoughts
find a light, bright, humorous side
have fun
break through our limiting beliefs about our potential
break through barriers of fear and mistrust
remember how to play
create energy
demonstrate the need for playfulness for creativity
take ourselves out of the same old rut
lift ourselves out of our limits, boundaries, or beliefs for problem-
   solving
keep ourselves open to learning
break through negatively held perceptions of self

Using the Bright Side tools accomplishes these goals, as does playing games. At a Bright Side seminar, a group of executives at AT&T/Bell Labs played the problem-solving game of nine dots. The participants are asked to draw only four connected straight lines to connect all nine dots, without lifting the pencil from the paper.

.   .   .

.   .   .

.   .   .

It is only after looking outside of the nine dots that the problem is solved. Solutions that I see repeatedly:

Ooops! All nine dots need to be connected.

Ooops! What about the middle dot?

Ooops! What about the side dots?

Ooops! Please use only four straight and connected lines.

Over and over, participants try familiar paths of dot connecting. It is only after actually going beyond the obvious—the boundaries of the nine dots, that there is a solution, a creative insight. One solution follows.

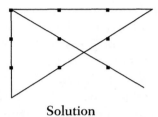

Solution

After the managers worked together as a team for nine-dot problem-solving, the team leader introduced a toss game using fruit and bottles of bubbles. The team was instructed to keep lowering the time it took to toss all items to each other in a specific pattern. The final time to accomplish this tossing game, in a consecutive pattern, was two seconds. In a lively and fun manner, the team clearly exhibited these cooperative teamwork traits:

- Taking risks
- Communication
- Interaction
- Facilitation of each other's efforts
- Utilization of each other's ideas
- Acceptance and support
- Trust
- Absence of fear of failure
- Good listening skills
- Cooperative intentions
- Absence of fear of making a mistake
- Absence of fear of foolishness
- Liking each other
- "Letting go" of the negative
- Openness and sharing of ideas
- Experimenting with new ideas
- Positive feedback and coaching

In fact, research shows that cooperative efforts result in higher productivity than interpersonal competitiveness.

How starved adults are for wellness, play, and fun-filled opportunities in their work environment. So often we confuse play and fun with the sports that we enjoy. When we play together and when we laugh together, we build relationships. We connect to each other in a deep way, without barriers. That is what creates a real sense of heart and spirit within an organization.

It has taken people longer than necessary to get where they are today because they have not learned the skills needed for positive habits. Thus, it is necessary to learn new ideas by repetition and to use as many tools as possible to form deep new patterns of behavior and thinking.

Bright Side tools are often provided as a simple method to reinforce learning and positive action. Desired behavior must be rewarded. Playful tools bring joy to the work environment. Clever, creative, novel approaches break through tired rituals of behavior and training. They increase productivity. In some Bright Side presentations, people often are skeptical about using the tools at first. You can almost see them saying to themselves, *This is silly.* That's a normal reaction to change. But by the end of the session, they often report feeling exuberant and learning a lot. These exercises allow people the opportunity to experiment with change in nonthreatening ways.

17

Coloring Out of the Lines

Boundaries begin even before we learn to color within the lines. I'm reminded of the lyrics to "Flowers Are Red," by Harry Chapin:

The little boy went first day in school, he gets crayons and he
   started to draw,
He put colors all over the paper, all colors was what he saw.
And the teacher said, "What you doing young man?"
"I'm painting flowers," he said.
She said, "It's not the time for art, young man, and flowers are
   green and red."
But the little boy said, "There are all colors in the rainbow, so
   many colors in the morning sun.
So many colors in the flower, and I see every one."
Well, the teacher said, "You're sassy. There are ways that things
   should be and you'll paint flowers the way they are, so repeat
   after me."
And she said, "Flowers are red young man, green leaves are green.
There's no need to see flowers any other way than the way they
   always have been seen."

But the little boy said again, "There are so many colors in the rain-
bow, so many colors in the morning sun.
So many colors in the flower, and I see every one."
Well, the teacher put him in a corner. She said, "It's for your own
good.
And you won't come out until you get it right and responding like
you should."
Well, finally he got lonely, frightened thoughts filled his head.
And he went up to that teacher and this is what he said.
And he said, "Flowers are red, and green leaves are green.
There's no need to see flowers any other way than the way they
always have been seen."
Of course, time flew like it always does. They moved to another
town.
And the little boy went to another school. This is what he found.
The teacher there is smiling. She said, "Painting should be fun.
And there are so many colors in the flower, so let's use every one."
But that little boy painted flowers of rose, green and red.
And when the teacher asked him why, this is what he said.
And he said, "Flowers are red, and green leaves are green.
There's no need to see flowers any other way than the way they
always have been seen."[8]

Those words so poignantly address the loss of our unique, colorful, creative self. How sad that our risk-taking wonder, creativity,
and intuition are stifled and snuffed out! Many people get caught
up in believing that creativity is only given to an anointed few. How
mistaken they are! In the rush for perfection, we ruin the creative
process, which is built on improvisation.

Limited thinking begins in kindergarten when we are each given
the same picture to color. "Stay within the lines," we are told. That
is how we internalize the concept of conformity, of being the same.
We learn that it's risky to show individual differences erupting from
our creative minds, and thus we learn not to trust our own ideas.
Our culture subtly encourages our young people as well as our adult
workers not to be risk-takers, not to rock the boat, to be content as
followers. In fact, what is needed to increase innovation and productivity are risk-takers with imagination.

While speaking at an American Society of Interior Designers (ASID) convention, I engaged in wonderful conversations with designers and design students. One woman, Joan, originally a CPA, left her job to study design. That was a courageous move for her. As a kindergartner, her teacher actually yelled at her for being too slow and meticulous in creating her artwork.

Her first childhood conditionings were: "Art isn't fun. I can't draw." Those faulty conclusions became the unstable foundation for her next set of beliefs: "To be a designer, one must be able to draw. I can't draw." It took thirty years for her to break out of those myths. She learned being an artist isn't a requirement for being a designer. She learned instead that we can all be artists. It is simply a function of drawing loose-flowing lines—the freeing kind, not the coloring-in-the-box kind.

In their book, *Build Your Brain Power,* Dr. Arthur Winter and Ruth Winter write, "Creativity is one of the most marvelous products of the 'fit' brain." They go on to quote Dr. Frederick M. Flack, a psychiatrist, who said,

> Creativity is not just a product or an act, but a way of viewing and reacting in new and constructive ways. You have to adapt and readapt to your environment, at home, at work, and in your relationships. You also have to trust your intuition. Intuition is quite different than impulsiveness. It involves perceiving something along preconscious routes frequently bypassing ordinary logic. It is often an artist's or a writer's intuition that makes masterpieces.[9]

As we can see from his emphasis, we have a major need to create. Flack also maintains, "The person who is creative has the ability to envision things in different ways to have a fresh outlook."

The right hemisphere of the brain is the seat of creativity, intuition, and imagination. Our creative mind is vital because it is the source of new ideas. These are critical to professional or personal problem-solving, inventions, and discoveries. In *Build Your Brain Power,* the Winters offer these exercises to stimulate the brain for creativity:

- Name all the kinds of dogs you can eat.
- Fill in: Her eyes were as green as _____.

- Write, within three minutes, every word you can think of that begins with the letter *y*.
- Make as many different things as you can out of circles and squares.

The following creativity-enhancing techniques from *Build Your Brain Power* are based on the work of Dr. Flack, Dr. Morris Stein, and other experts:

Prepare yourself. Do as much reading and talking as you can about what you want to create—a solution, a picture, a new approach to a business. Do your homework.

Incubate. We all want quick solutions, but when the answers don't come right away, put the thought aside. Let it simmer in your subconscious. At a later point, perhaps a week or a month later, there will be a breakthrough.

Illuminate. In cartoons, this is depicted by a lightbulb over the head. It is the point when the breakthrough occurs. You let it happen. Something pops into your head and you say, "Ah, that's a good idea."

Test. Now that you've come up with the creative solution, you have to apply it. If there is a new way to handle your marriage, for example, put it into practice. If you have a new way of creating a sculpture, do it. Dr. Flack says that nobody gets the Nobel Prize for a new idea. One gets it for testing the idea and showing how it works.

Distance yourself. You can do this merely by changing your clothes or the room in which you are working. You can take a "mental excursion" by thinking about a pleasant trip you took or a place you'd like to go. Picture something far removed from your ordinary interests or work.

Have a variety of leisure pursuits. Don't spend your leisure time at one avocation, such as tennis or watching TV. Get a variety of experiences. Meet new people. Read new books. Primarily, leisure should relax you. It is hard to be creative when you are tense. And by avoiding routine—tennis only or TV only—you gain the stimuli of various people and environments, and you use a variety of your muscles and talents. Variety is fertilizer for creativity.

Find security. It is very difficult to be creative if you are worried about survival. You need to find someone on whom you can depend. Anxiety blocks the free flow of creativity.

Don't play a role. If you select a role such as the man-in-the-gray-flannel-suit or the superwoman, you get locked in and can't do things another way.

Choose your associates carefully. If you associate with people who are constantly tearing you down and criticizing you, you won't be able to create.

Don't be afraid to be alone. If you are to be creative, you need time to listen to your inner self instead of someone or something else.

Try to turn down your motor. You need some inactive and quiet time to let your thought processes work. That means daydreaming, a form of mental activity frowned upon by parents and teachers; yet it is useful and may open up new channels. You can also reminisce and allow past successes to flow through your mind for reevaluation.

Keep a pencil and notebook handy. You can capture fleeting ideas that may later prove to be valuable. You never know what connections may be made between what is novel to you and what you ordinarily have to do.

Find your best time. You are influenced by your biological rhythm. There is a time of day or night when you are at your best. You probably know it, but if you want to make sure, it is probably the time when your body temperature is highest.

Find your best place. Try to remember where you got your best ideas. Some people like to think in a warm bathtub and others while walking or while working with their hands.

Write or tape your frustrations. When you are feeling frustrated or tied up in knots and the ideas won't come, write or record what is bothering you. It will help "clear the decks" for action.

Farm your brain. Verbalize or write down as many ideas as you can dig out of your brain. Let your mind wander and consider all sorts of solutions. You can help yourself till the fertile soil by making analogies, for example, "I want to paint a better picture, but it is like squeezing the last bit of toothpaste from the tube."

Creative dawning. In this technique (which has been called other names), you put your goal in the center, or "sun," and then try to think of as many ideas—no matter how crazy—as you can that could help you achieve your goal. Put those ideas in the rays around your dawning sun.

Defer judgment. Really listen to your own thoughts, but don't judge your ideas right away. Don't say, "That's foolish" or "That won't work." By offering negative adjectives, you block the flow of ideas. Keep coming up with solutions, no matter how crazy they may sound. Quantity will eventually produce quality.

Don't be afraid to make mistakes. If you fail, learn what doesn't work. Try a new approach. If you are not failing, you are not being very creative, because new trails are unmarked and full of pitfalls.

Don't make excuses. Age, infirmity, and lack of time or money are frequent reasons given for not being able to create. They are rarely valid. Picasso at age ninety-one kept art supplies by his bed in case he awoke during the night and had a good idea. He could then capture it on paper. George Bernard Shaw wrote "The Millionairess" in his eighties. The output of composer Gabriel Faure (1845–1924) increased in quantity and quality during his eighth decade of life, even in the face of severe sensory impairment.[10]

I absolutely love my children's *Anti-Coloring Book,* by Susan Striker. Such books encourage fresh and original thinking. Some of the exercises are frivolous and fun, others stimulating and challenging. Here are some examples:

- Build a fort out of snow.
- Construct a factory for the kind of business you would like to own.
- You are very rich; erect a luxury tent for camping in the woods.

- The old train station was torn down, and you have been asked to design a new one.
- Build a tree house where you can go to be alone.

Go ahead and try it. Using all of the colors you have available, draw a picture of a personal vision that would give purpose and meaning to your life.

Part 5

Practice the
Bright Side Virtues

The media, particularly television and motion pictures, bombard us with images that the mind assimilates and interprets as reality. In fact, at the University of Michigan Institutes for Social Research, Professor Hazel Markus draws a connection between the media and our possible selves insofar as we draw from a pool of images we see around us. Unfortunately, these images can sweep us into a realm of behavior that is frequently violent, greedy, sexually oriented, and plastic.

Working at the University of California at Berkeley, Richard A. Lazarus, a National Institute on Aging grantee, found that the frequency of irritations of everyday life—traffic jams, cancelled appointments, tight schedules—as well as of uplifting experiences of everyday life is a more accurate predictor of psychological and physical health than are major events of one's life.

In this final section, we'll examine how good leaders work in these difficult times and harsh environments, helping mold the inner soil of their people. We'll explore how they help others transcend normal human fears and bring out the best that each has to offer. As the diagram suggests, the nurturing of people's cores breaks down resistance to learning and along with it, self-imposed limits. It leads people and their organizations toward continuous self-improvement, team and personal effectiveness and, finally, customer delight.

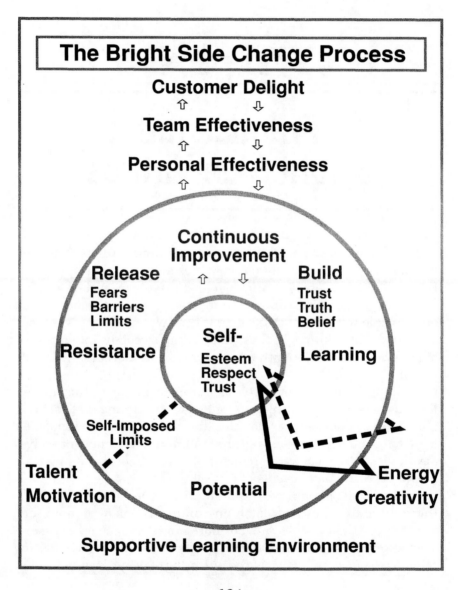

18

Getting from Fear to Trust

In terms of sheer pervasiveness, as well as in the far-reaching damage it can do to people's spirits, perhaps no human emotion can compete with fear. It leaves a path of disastrous consequences.

Fear knows no professional category. It knows no age. Fear inhibits CEOs, machine operators, children, secretaries, parents, and teachers.

There are many kinds of fear—fear of failure, fear of self, fear of appearing foolish, fear of the unknown, and fear of change. It feeds on itself, as depicted in the poem "Knots," by R. D. Laing.

> Jack is afraid of Jill
> Jill is afraid of Jack
> Jack is more afraid of Jill
> if Jack thinks
> that Jill thinks
> that Jack is afraid of Jill
> Jill is more afraid of Jack
> if Jill thinks
> that Jack thinks
> that Jill is afraid of Jack

Since Jack is afraid
that Jill will think that
Jack is afraid
Jack pretends that
Jack is not afraid of Jill
So that Jill will be more afraid of Jack
and since Jill is afraid
that Jack will think that
Jill is afraid
Jill pretends that
Jill is not afraid of Jack
Jack tries to make Jill afraid
by not being afraid of Jill
and Jill tries to make Jack afraid
by not being afraid of Jack
The more Jack is afraid of Jill
the more frightened is Jack that
Jill will think
that Jack is afraid
etc., etc.[11]

Fear of Failure

Perhaps the paramount fear is the fear of failure. It causes us to do less or settle for less in order to avoid shame, humiliation, or pain. The most common reason for a person's failure is not making a wrong decision, but not making any decision. And fear can give rise to a lack of trust in one's own ability to think, to learn, and to decide.

Fear of Self

I was paralyzed by fear when the domestic machine tool industry collapsed. I felt vulnerable, like a crab having molted its hard shell. I only knew my professional mask. Once that was dropped, I was afraid of discovering my deeper identity. I feared that the real me couldn't possibly be acceptable or worthy. I feared that I had no value without the identity of my work.

I remember being on the shore of the Chesapeake Bay, allowing waves and sand to sweep over my feet. Suddenly I was trapped by the tide, paralyzed by inertia. That is what fear does to us.

Fear of Appearing Foolish

In much the same way, Jack Smith, the president and CEO of Neway Anchorlok in Muskegon, Michigan, decided that his organization—a manufacturer of truck braking systems—needed a new level of energy. So at one company Christmas party, he picked up a banjo and began playing.

More fundamentally, though, at a meeting with the entire organization, after explaining his emerging vision for the company, he invited anyone who was willing to go along with him to stand up. He created such passion and excitement that everyone got to his or her feet.

Smith admires a metaphor used by his brother-in-law, a business consultant, who draws the parallel between old and new organizations by comparing symphonies and jazz bands. In symphonies, there is a single leader, the conductor, and the outcome of the music is pre-ordained. This is similar to an old-fashioned organization. But in jazz, everyone is a leader and everyone makes music. And the result is complete improvisation. This is similar to a new organization.

It's difficult to become good leaders if we fear making fools of ourselves. Many of us can be overly serious about our work and our personal lives, unable to bring the notion of creative play to our work. Albert Einstein wrote about the freedom to play with concepts and ideas as being a vital source of creativity. But those of us from dysfunctional families often tend to look at play as inappropriate, especially in serious arenas like work. Yet the ability to play, even if it appears foolish, encourages risk-taking and creative thought.

Fear of the Unknown

We often avoid situations when we feel fearful of or intimidated by unclear outcomes. We feel at risk when results are uncertain; it's safer to stay out of a dark cave. Turning around and going back to safety is more reassuring than going forward toward the unknown.

And yet, venturing into uncharted territory carries potentially great rewards. Victor Ide, formerly the human resources manager for a trucking company and now a Wal-Mart executive, tells it best in an experience he had in his friendship with David, a man who is deaf.

Victor and David met in St. Louis. At first, Victor wanted to avoid David because he represented the unknown. Victor was also afraid of making a fool of himself by trying to communicate with this deaf man. He preferred to avoid David, even though he knew sign language because of his mother's deafness.

Victor finally risked communicating with David. As a result, he grew in ways that benefited both himself and the company. Victor now takes advanced sign language classes and hires people with physical disabilities. And he is no longer afraid to address the issue of bringing disabled people into the work environment. After all, most of us are disabled in one way or another.

It is often easier and less painful to give up when faced with apparent obstacles. We are so comfortable with what is familiar. We can predict the outcome when we stay on the familiar course. But it's only through discomfort that we give birth to a new level of understanding. The pain shatters the old self and the old understanding that limits our potential. As the Bible says, "I tell you, most solemnly, unless a wheat grain falls on the ground and dies, it remains only a single grain; but if it dies, it yields a rich harvest" (John 12:24 JB).

Fear of Change

To grow, we must be willing to let go of the old self by letting go of cherished notions. This is the only way we can assimilate the new. But because of our traditional way of teaching and thinking about management, such dynamic change is often difficult. Frank Mosier, a retired senior officer of an international oil company, notes that until recently, many business school textbooks taught management techniques that imprison the workforce. These tactics grew, he says, out of the widely held conviction that people perform better when leadership is critical of them.

Mosier tells the story of a company, no longer in existence, where the chairman insisted on gathering his top managers for a mandatory, formal lunch, complete with assigned seating. No one was permitted to sit until the chairman rang a bell. Such extreme rigidity stems from our cultural addiction to control, power, and elitism—the very characteristics that have triggered the demise of the American spirit, impeding change and freezing people into fear and mediocrity.

Growth, learning, and change must be ongoing, even for already successful organizations and individuals. Success isn't an end, but rather the substance that can give rise to greater success. It is the "peak to peek principle" outlined by Robert H. Schuller. Having had a peak experience, one gets a glimpse of other opportunities and future potential.

Mosier points to a personal example of the need for change in the midst of success. After he had been CEO of a company, he realized that his successful track record led him to assume that he knew what would or would not work and that he was becoming no smarter or more creative as a result. He eventually invited workers, their supervisors, and middle managers to suggest ideas. He solicited their input by telling them that they had ideas about how to organize the work that were probably more effective than what they were already doing.

While the frontline people responded with an outpouring of ideas, he recalls, their managers and supervisors became defensive. Their fear, which is universal, sprang from a natural desire to look good. Rather than being perceived as the conduit through which good ideas must pass from the shop floor to the board room, they wanted to sell ideas to top management as their own. But Mosier contends that would have been demotivating to the frontline workers. If people are not given credit for their ideas, he says, the organization breeds yes-people who do as little as they can and won't go the extra mile.

In his nationally syndicated radio series, *Our Changing World,* the late Earl Nightingale once told a beautiful story of a man who, while mining for diamonds in Africa, sells his farm in search of the ultimate success. He ends his life broken and penniless, never having found a mine. Yet, on the very farm he sold, a great diamond mine was later discovered. As Mosier found, often the ingredients of success are close at hand; but we can only see them if we can free ourselves from the limited thinking produced by the fear of change.

Fear freezes us, physically and mentally. According to family counselor Virginia Satir, "When your body feels tight, your brain often freezes right along with your tight body, and so your thinking becomes limited as well."[12]

Admitting Fear

Yet fear can also propel us to greatness. My friend and client Jack Kahl, the chairman of Manco, thinks we are only truly living when we have the feeling of being out on thin ice. And, he says, "I'm glad I'm on this ice."

He believes corporate leaders mask their own fear by pretending they are in charge, thus protecting their image of power and control. Kahl believes, instead, that leaders must be role models for risk-taking and willingness to change. Only they can lead the way in an organization, and yet he estimates that fewer than one in twenty corporate leaders are willing to change, learn, and grow. "There is more lip service than action, keeping the group in authority in control of others," he says. "The greatest learning disability is the human wiring. It is the software inside that is the barrier." Kahl says what most only think: "I'm a little kid inside. I'm scared."

Kahl surrounds himself with great teachers, high-fiber human beings. Two of his teachers were Sam Walton, the dynamic and humble chairman of Wal-Mart who died recently, and Socrates. Over Kahl's office door is a quote from Socrates that speaks eloquently to the issues he addresses: "One thing only I know, and that is that I know nothing."

Because the boss himself admits it, everyone at Manco can freely admit they don't know everything. Kahl believes that if he wants his people to learn, he has to be the first to show his willingness to be retrained. A willingness to humble oneself demonstrates a person's real, internal strength. Kahl credits Sam Walton with this idea. After all, how can people feel empowered if their leader believes he is intrinsically smarter than they are?

Trust

When we resist change out of fear of the unknown, we're inviting danger to our jobs, our families, even the future of our country. Fear is useless, Scripture reminds us. What is needed is trust. But how do we get there? Perhaps through trisking. *Trisk* is a word I learned from wellness expert Dr. John Travis. It weds two words, *trust* and *risk*. Trust plus risk is *trisk*. Trust is strengthened through risk-taking, not necessarily on the physical level, but rather on the mental, emotional, and spiritual level. Tom Finley, human resources executive at Rubbermaid, believes people's performance will be mediocre unless they are motivated to take risks and learn. "This is more critical in today's global marketplace where we are far more dependent on the initiative of people."

Often, we can take the initial step toward internal trust-building by doing or saying things we have never done or said before, particularly in the face of fear. Energy and confidence are increased when we let go of the defensive masks of self-protection.

Cleveland attorney and venture capitalist Ted Garver, for example, maintains that the primary function of an attorney is to protect people who cannot trust one another. He compares this lack of trust to that of cavemen, who were continually faced with the fear of death by predatory animals. Today, he says, a similar lack of trust permeates our business relationships.

This quagmire of defensive communication and behavior dominates business environments. At Garick, a $7-million national wholesale landscape supply company based in Cleveland, one manager estimated that as much as 75 percent of a person's energy is spent on defensive behavior and defensive communication. What a productivity loss!

Where trust flourishes, good results will follow. This can only happen in an environment that encourages free communication, where people feel safe in expressing their thoughts, creative ideas, and emotions. For many, this type of environment is foreign, and they don't expect it in the workplace. But it's the path to increased trust, self-esteem, and personal empowerment at work as well as in personal relationships.

In order to build trust, we must first trust ourselves. And in order to do that, a lot of internal healing is necessary. How many past negatives are we holding on to that dramatically interfere with productivity and trust? A loving inner dialogue makes us less critical and more receptive. We should be willing to let go of our fear-based, defensive, destructive behavior.

19

Truth—No Pain, No Gain

Begin to think about the people who have most influenced your life. As you review their character, honesty will probably be one of the qualities you most treasured.

Avoidance is always more painful than confronting the truth. As I work with people and organizations throughout the country, I recognize the misery avoidance creates. The consequences range from third-hand gossip that places people in the midst of half-truths and makes them unable to do their jobs because the real issues are unclear, to bad feelings that only the truth will alleviate. As John (8:32 KJV) says, "And ye shall know the truth, and the truth shall make you free." This is not truth at all costs, but truth based on the desire for personal growth and mutual trust.

Truth with Others

I recognize that it is difficult for most of us to honestly communicate. Yet the most powerful gift that we can give another human being is truth. Communicating with honesty can build not only mutual trust, but also our own self-trust and self-respect.

For instance, at Zaclon, one production team very effectively and truthfully addresses its issues or problems without management supervision. Another team confronted a coworker about his work ethic.

There are some important guidelines for honest communication. First, we must carefully explore our intent behind our honesty. Is our intent to nurture growth, or is our honesty driven by selfishness? A selfless intent is an important requirement. Kindness and compassion are also essential. Realizing that we can be both kind and honest provides a new mental picture. When our intent is pure, kindness is less difficult. Kind, honest disclosures can strengthen relationships by helping both parties break out of old paradigms.

Another guideline is to suggest an alternative along with the honest feedback. Be careful to explain that the feedback comes from your point of view and that your interest is to help. Feedback and encouragement must be honest and genuine, never manipulative or insincere.

The following additional suggestions can be helpful in setting up honest dialogue.

- Eliminate the attitude of "You are wrong and I am right." That is adversarial and can provoke defensive communication.
- Be patient.
- Be willing to listen with your heart, moving out of the state of rational logic which will certainly create a judgmental mindset.
- Eliminate blame and negative language.
- Avoid using honest feedback as retaliation for anger, annoyance, or vengeance.

Giving and receiving feedback requires listening. Listening requires hard work and energy. However, it may be one of the truest forms of showing someone we care. Positive, honest communication is challenging and requires practice. Seize the opportunity to practice. These are skills to be developed; they are not talents. Be willing to accept other people's varying levels of proficiency in this area.

Through honest communication, experiences, ideas, and creativity begin to flourish. People stop hiding behind a myriad of lies and can begin to focus their energy on life-giving activities. As Tom Finley, human resources executive at Rubbermaid, says, "Trust and harmony can only exist in an organization where leaders are more concerned about truth than the deceit of covering their tracks."

Truth gives others an opportunity to improve. Often we learn of a person losing a job, unaware of an employer's dissatisfaction; or of promotions not provided because change was required. Truth would have given those people a great opportunity to grow beyond their current level of performance.

The Hackett & Arnold real estate company's leader, Candy Lum, is a courageous woman who puts truth into action. She continuously gives feedback to her agents and managers about their performance, noting where changes or improvements are required. While confronting some issues is not always an easy task, Lum addresses the most sensitive situations with love and honesty, preserving the dignity of her associates by giving them time and space to implement her suggestions or to explore other internal or external opportunities.

Truth with Yourself

Dr. Scott Peck, in *The Road Less Traveled*, writes, "What makes life difficult is that the process of confronting and solving problems is a painful one. It is only because of problems that we grow mentally and spiritually. It is through the pain of confronting and resolving problems that we learn."[13] Benjamin Franklin wrote, "Those things that hurt, instruct." We should learn to welcome problems rather than avoid them.

For many of us, our main problem is truth about ourselves. Yet we need self-truth in order to have integrity in our lives and work. It is the seed required to grow healthy and honest communication. Accepting and addressing truth reflect self-respect, allowing us to respect others.

Gary Trinetti, the young president of the Garick Corp., a wholesale landscaper, is an extraordinary example of what can happen when a person confronts the truth about his or her life. In high school, he was such a disruptive student that two teachers asked him not to come to class anymore. He graduated with a 1.8 grade point average. He dropped out of college. Working for his father and uncle, he was told, "We don't pay you to think. Grab a shovel." Every idea he and his brother had was "stupid." In their father's company, they weren't allowed to think.

Now, however, Trinetti has grown a company. His brother, who was also once a common laborer in the family business, works with him, running a division. At Gary's lowest point, brought about by his girlfriend's rejection, his poor academic performance, and the limits heaped on him by his family business, he miraculously realized he could choose. He could choose a different life! What courage to accept responsibility for his problems and predicament—it was his own self-truth. When he went back to college, he became the best student he could be. What he overcame is the impetus for his own encouragement of his employees and his continued attitude of teachability.

Moving out of denial and confronting truth can be painful and difficult. In my own life, the most freeing experiences have been ones of accepting the truth. I experienced devastating pain when I avoided the reality of my life in the machine tool industry. Today, I seek opportunities for improvement. I don't always like what I hear; yet I know I can change and do something differently.

My children keep me on the path of truth, letting me know when I have done something hurtful. My clients keep me on a path of truth by letting me know when I am helpful and when I am not. In fact, I always ask at the end of a Bright Side program or coaching session how I have helped, how I haven't, and what I need to do differently to be of greater service. And God also keeps me on the path of truth, with his Spirit of truth, by pricking my conscience, filling me with understanding, insight, and wisdom.

20

Spiritually Centered Leadership

Contrary to the reigning ethos of Wall Street in the '80s, as a long-term motivator for leaders as well as for those they lead, greed is a proven dud. Thankfully, many have turned elsewhere for a set of guiding principles.

An increasing number of leaders in America have embraced spiritually-centered management, apparently in the same spirit as Matthew 16:26: "What good will it be for a man if he gains the whole world, yet forfeits his soul?" Replacing greed with love, these courageous people have moved from the traditional overseer model to that of the servant. Love, as described in the Book of Corinthians, is patience, kindness, and rejoicing in the truth. And when applied both to communicating with the internal organization and to serving customers, this model can work wonders.

Jack Dannemiller, the president of the Cleveland-based manufacturing company Bearings, Inc., says the Book of Proverbs provides the best management advice he's ever found. In my work with other spiritually-centered—and by the way quite successful—managers, I have found that they share a few basic characteristics.

147

Rather than superficially modeling themselves after how they think successful leaders should dress or talk or comport themselves, these leaders exemplify these guidelines:

Never grow tired of doing good. These leaders always find better ways to communicate, to make life easier and more enjoyable for others. They continually strive to serve.

Listen with their heart. Rather than enjoying the sound of their own voices all the time, the spiritually-centered leader appreciates the wisdom inherent in Notre Dame football coach Lou Holtz's observation: "When I talk, I'm not learning anything. The only time I'm learning is when I'm listening." These leaders listen closely not out of grudging duty but out of an authentic appreciation for what others have to teach.

Cheerlead and champion customer delight. They role-model ways to provide customer surprise, joy, and delight.

Always try to find what's good. Whether striving for continual improvement by discovering what competitors are doing better, or recognizing the good actions of coworkers, family members, or friends, spiritually-centered leaders have an intense focus on the good.

Uphold people. Rather than leading by intimidation, as business managers have traditionally been taught, these leaders inspire by building their employees' self-esteem. They have more faith in the potential of people than in the problem.

Offer forgiveness. These leaders try to move out of judgment and into understanding.

Have integrity. Good leaders have little gap in their values. They don't say one thing and act differently. They align their actions with their stated beliefs, wherever that may lead.

Offer constant encouragement and praise. As the theologian Doris Donnelly says in her book, *Spiritual Fitness*, "Praise begins by letting the other just 'be.' That kind of being presupposes the ability to forget oneself. It belongs to perceptive, open, and truthful people capable of admiring and adoring others."[14] Spiritually-based leaders never hesitate to recognize and encourage excellence in others, because they have no trouble submerging their own egos in pursuit of group goals.

Leaders answering to these exacting specifications are becoming slightly less rare. "Our company's foundation is our belief in God," says Donna Freeman, a partner in the Cincinnati-based Culver-Freeman insurance agency and president of the National Organization of Women Life Underwriters. "We are always going beyond traditional expectations. We focus on the person, knowing the business and profit will come later. To us, it is essential to develop trust. We live through life-and-death issues with our clients."

Similarly, Sheila Gallagher-Nadeau, human relations leader for Forest City Enterprises, has found that the path to profit can't come at the expense of people. "To uphold the human factor," she says, "we must be aware of the spirit of God existing in all people. My first priority is to uphold everyone in my company."

She recalls struggling at a prayer retreat to find her own personal integrity. By facing her inner emptiness, she experienced God's unconditional love and was spiritually reborn. After accepting the truth about her own life, she then began to narrow the gap between her values and her behavior. That experience now motivates her to help others heal and to bring integrity to the workplace. "Integrity can only exist with self-integrity and belief in God," she says.

As the writer Kahlil Gibran grasped in his powerful book, *The Prophet,* people who work with dignity and love reap bountiful rewards.

> You have been told that life is darkness, and in your weariness you echo what was said by the weary. And I say that life is indeed darkness save when there is urge. And all urge is blind save when there is knowledge. And all knowledge is vain save when there is work. And all work is empty save when there is love. And when you work with love you bind yourself to yourself, and to one another, and to God.[15]

Wal-Mart founder Sam Walton explained in his book, *Made in America,* "While I was at Missouri, I was elected president of the Burall Bible Class—a huge class made up of students from both Missouri and Stephens colleges. Growing up, I had always gone to church and Sunday school every Sunday. It was an important part of my life. I don't know if I was a religious person, but I always felt like the church was important."[16]

Walton told Manco chairman Jack Kahl that his most important contribution was helping to improve the self-esteem of others. In fact, Kahl says, Walton believed in Kahl's potential long before he himself did. Walton's belief in Kahl afforded Manco astounding opportunities. As he often did, Walton listened to a suggestion from a Wal-Mart shopper, this time for home-office products. This spurred Wal-Mart's decision to consolidate vendors for an entire mailing- and shipping-supplies program, something no one had ever done before. Manco seized the opportunity to serve Wal-Mart and its customers. In four months, Manco developed and shipped a complete assortment of mailing products as part of a package that was an industry first: CareMail.

Pete Wilzbach of ISSC considered the priesthood as a young man. But today, he finds an outlet for his deep spirituality by helping challenge, motivate, and teach the sixteen hundred people who report to him.

In the ISSC newsletter, Wilzbach once referred to a Scripture passage.

> You are the light of the world. A city on a hill cannot be hidden. Neither do people light a lamp and put it under a bowl. Instead they put it on its stand, and it gives light to everyone in the house. In the same way, let your light shine before men, that they may see your good deeds and praise your Father in heaven.
>
> Matthew 5:14–16

Wilzbach's own paraphrase of this passage was, "Don't hide your candle under a bush, let it shine for the whole world to see." Wilzbach's own candle is ever on display, generously lighting the path for others. He strives to create "a family environment filled with love, fun and accomplishment," he says.

As a twenty-four-year IBM veteran, he was trained in a traditionally restrictive, buttoned-down management environment, where executives were frowned upon for wearing anything but the customary white shirts. But when ISSC was formed in the early

'90s to move more quickly and aggressively than the larger organization could in competing for business in the highly competitive data-processing outsourcing sector, even the parent company knew that the new unit would have to be managed differently if it were to succeed.

"You'd be hard-pressed to find a white shirt around here now. We've mostly gone casual in dress. But for those of us who still wear suits and ties, we don't have many white shirts left," Wilzbach says. As he explains it, "The business we are in involves taking tremendous risk and signing up to do the impossible. We often are asked to take over an efficiently run data center and operate it for half the cost. The pressure this puts on our people is tremendous, and the rate of change is almost chaotic. Adding to this is the constant evolution of technology and software. There are no technical classes that can train people how to succeed in this area, because every situation is unique. Instead, we need to train people to have a positive attitude and confidence in their abilities and assume that they will create the right technical solution."

At the same time, in order to encourage team spirit and drive home the importance of service, he injected fun into the workplace. "The managers needed to lighten up as we went to self-directed work teams. This can't be all doom and gloom," he says. Thus were born various celebrations such as Employee Appreciation Week, during which managers served a pizza lunch to seven hundred people. For IBM, where most of ISSC's employees had previously worked, "this was a big leap."

Wilzbach's people-first philosophy was put to the ultimate test when cost-cutting measures threatened the jobs of twenty of his people. But instead of simply surrendering to the inevitable by lopping off the positions, Wilzbach challenged the imperiled team to create its own new business and in so doing save their jobs. Freeing them to be inventive and giving them a target date, they eventually emerged with a bold new product, now on the market: a CD-ROM version of the New Bible Library, the first computerized-data library to offer a search-and-retrieval system.

What an inspiring example of spiritually centered leadership. Rather than merely commanding a certain outcome, Wilzbach opened the door so that his people might glimpse previously unimagined outcomes. Endowed with that simple permission from above, they accomplished the extraordinary, with tangible rewards for everyone. Just imagine what an entire economy of such leaders and organizations might accomplish.

21

Champions

Defensive, fearful behavior can sometimes contaminate entire groups. The wounded inner child acts defensively and destructively. Adults who act like this are like overgrown kids with unmet needs. They can be belligerent, stubborn, and hostile. Sometimes the hostility is masked by hurtful, toxic humor. The negative behavior is so powerfully contaminating that the energy of an entire group is drained, and soon there is a negative consensus.

I have observed negative behavior in a number of organizations. One of two things occurs: Enlightened leaders move forward, empowering the positive, imprisoning the negative, and trusting that while change is slow, positive behavior will eventually be effective; or unenlightened leaders stop moving forward, in an effort to appease the naysayers and minimize discomfort, thereby empowering the negative and defeating the positive.

Enlightened leaders are champions of change. The main way in which we can encourage higher standards is to expose people to champions.

Champions can be found in the rank and file, too. On a trip to New York, I encountered a delightful taxi driver whom I shall never forget. I was en route to the Newark Airport in New Jersey after a

153

workshop. He was filled with joy and enthusiasm. He told me about his daytime job as a postman, referring to his customers as his family. He told me that when people were on vacations, he made sure their houses were safe. If he delivered packages when they were gone, he would leave a note inside the mailbox informing them where they could find their packages upon their return.

On one delivery he realized the resident was not well. He called the emergency squad and had the man taken to a nearby community hospital. He later phoned to see how the man was doing.

For an elderly couple that have difficulty moving around, he brings the mail right into the house, walking into whichever room they happen to be in. I was fascinated hearing his stories. It was late at night and he had worked a full day as a postman, walking from house to house. Yet here he was, so alive, alert, and happy.

Studies have shown that in the process of giving, we actually feel better. We elevate our level of endorphins, which are natural mood-elevating biochemicals. And that's the effect I saw in this man. He sounded joyful and alert. In delivering the mail, he acted as though he was on commission, with each good deed increasing his income.

I encountered another champion while traveling the East Coast. I had finished three days of presentations in Washington, D.C., and was traveling to New York City. True to form it was close to take-off time when I arrived at the airport. One skycap must have noticed how I scurried, for he announced that he would give me service like I had never had before.

What could this service be like? As time was precious, I did not have the luxury to ask him. Rather, I said that I would appreciate that kind of service. With a huge smile, he grabbed my briefcase and garment bag and asked for my ticket. He whisked me to the check-in counter and checked me in. Then he suggested that I follow him. He bubbled with enthusiasm. He walked me directly to my gate. Yes! Yes! That was service like I have never had before.

Workers such as this New Jersey postman and Washington skycap deserve to be honored, not only for the good job they do, but for the tremendous role-modeling for customer service they provide. This cab driver and skycap were champion performers, just as Allison Roe was a champion performer.

I'm reminded of the topic of champion role-modeling whenever I think of one special lunchtime experience I had. My friend and I planned to have lunch around Christmas one year, and she suggested an Italian restaurant that was on the near west side of Cleveland. Upon our arrival, we were greeted by a parking attendant whose welcoming smile provided an instant clue that we were in for a special experience. We were welcomed by Tony, the owner, who recognized my friend, much to her delight. The enormous restaurant was packed. I quickly checked out the food, which looked outstanding. I then knew lunch would be an adventure.

But the scrumptious food was surpassed by acts of warmth and kindness. For dessert, the owner sent over homemade lemon ice and elegant Italian cookies. Then he sent us out the door with two loaves of bread, baked on the premises. Feeling treasured, we were once again greeted by the parking attendants, who were interested in knowing what we ate and how we liked it. With enthusiasm, they described their favorite dishes.

In this case, parking attendants, usually considered minor players in the restaurant business, set the stage for caring and reflected the same love, passion, and positive energy as Tony, the owner and their leader. My friend and I had a wonderful adventure because of the caring conveyed by the entire team. I've never had a more unforgettable dining experience. I yearn to return, all because of the standards set by one caring man who made me feel special and whose philosophy filtered throughout his organization.

That experience stood in sharp contrast to an afternoon at a prestigious Cleveland-area shopping mall. After returning from shopping and dining at this mall, I waited and waited for a parking attendant. Finally, after a ten-minute wait, I was told they could not find my keys. After much scrambling, the keys were found, but it still took some time for me to get my car. The promise of restitution he offered left me cold: "The next time you come, the parking is on us—and remember to come during hours I'm here." I haven't any desire to return. When will business discover that all contributions are important, and that the lasting ones can just as easily come from the lowest employee as from the person at the top? Companies that undervalue employees are only inviting themselves to undervalue customers.

22

Love

After moving to Cleveland, one of my first acquaintances in broadcasting was Jane Temple. Twenty years later, Jane, now married and the mother of three children, decided to leave her prestigious position at the local ABC-TV affiliate to spend more time with her family. She and I arranged a meeting to review broadcasting projects.

I looked forward to seeing Jane. When she arrived at my office, I immediately learned that in the past year, at forty, she had undergone open-heart surgery. Stunned and feeling vulnerable, I questioned her as to how the surgery had changed her life or her outlook.

Jane was open to sharing her heartfelt emotions, her feelings of mortality, her childhood experiences. For the first time in our twenty-year friendship, she shared details about herself. I learned that she had a family history of heart ailments that result in early death.

Jane had seen her own mother die at an early age from heart problems. Jane was raised by her aunt and uncle. I could picture her as a teenager, being cared for by this couple. However, she then shared with me that her relatives raised her from the time she was a very small child because her mother had never fully recovered from her divorce. Jane's revelation of herself, her identity, and her feelings

156

created a bond of trust that I had never before experienced with her. I felt safe.

"Jane," I asked softly, "did you know my sister Debby died of cancer this past year?" We looked directly at one another in mutual understanding of loss, protected by this new armor of trust. I realized that our friendship was rapidly deepening.

The trust that is so necessary to positive relationships sprang from her honest expression of her own vulnerability. Through trust and openness I had discovered the real Jane. She was authentic, very different from the image I had formed of her, or the image our media and culture had helped paint of her identity. I trusted her authenticity, not because it was perfection, but because it was truth.

This bridge of truth gave me the courage to tell Jane about my sister's death. Debby had breast cancer that metastasized throughout her body. It was a devastating and painful condition. Debby was a holy and extraordinary woman who thought about the welfare and happiness of others, never lamenting or feeling sorry for herself in the midst of her excruciating pain. She empathized with my son's diabetic condition, being sensitive to his daily blood tests and injections and the mood swings sometimes incurred during periods of high blood-sugar levels. She told him she understood his suffering because of what she was experiencing in the hospital with cancer. My son was completely touched by her compassion and sensitivity to his condition and overwhelmed, because he knew her cancerous condition caused pain far exceeding any discomfort he had experienced.

As I told Jane, Debby's love knew no boundaries. She was able to reach the deep inner spirit of every life she touched. It was through simplicity, truth, and love that she enriched others' lives—not through exterior images of power or control.

"Jane," I said, "Debby knew how to love." I explained that during the last two weeks of her life, she was quickly approaching a deep sleep. She spent much of her day with her eyes closed, yet fully conscious of her surroundings. One late afternoon, sitting next to her hospital bed, I told Debby that I knew she loved me, just by the way she looked at me. Without hesitation, Debby opened her eyes, wide and bright, and looked deeply, intently, and for a very long time directly into mine. Her look was so deep, loving, intense, and lasting that the intimacy was almost uncomfortable.

It made me aware, I told Jane, of how conditioned we are to accept less love and little or no intimacy, conditioned to pretend that the sexy images presented in the media embody love and intimacy. I knew Debby's look took great physical effort. She gave me the greatest present of all—the gift of love.

"I know exactly what you mean," Jane said. "I was at WEWS-TV when Dorothy Fuldheim had her stroke."

Dorothy Fuldheim was a Cleveland legend. A pioneer in broadcasting, highly opinionated and controversial, Dorothy broadcast live interviews and commentaries daily until the age of ninety. After a stroke at age ninety-three, she went into a coma. Jane was asked to organize a celebration for Dorothy's birthday. The station executives, who were not only Dorothy's employers, but also her friends and support group, wanted to bring Dorothy a birthday cake.

Jane remembers Dorothy being in the coma, apparently unaware of birthday well-wishers. Jane sat next to Dorothy and said, "Dorothy, we love you." Dorothy opened her eyes, looked directly at Jane, and said, "I hope so." Their deep inner core of love and spirit touched each other. Even for Dorothy Fuldheim, the beloved broadcaster, the most important thing at her life's end was to be loved.

As Jane related this to me, both of us were crying freely. Do we have to wait for life's end to discover that we are loved by others, and that we have loved others? The famous Dorothy and the simple and holy Debby, at the close of their physical lives, were concerned most about the lasting meaning of their lives. That lasting meaning was *love*—to be loved and to love. Since I have shared this experience with thousands of people, I have come to realize that this deep need for love, as described in those two women's lives, is universal.

Love Is . . .

"Do everything in love" (1 Cor. 16:14). But what is love? Is it that sensuous image constantly hurled at us from television, music, and movies? No, the best definition of love is again from the New Testament.

Love is patient, love is kind. It does not envy, it does not boast, it is not proud. It is not rude, it is not self-seeking, it is not easily angered, it keeps no record of wrongs. Love does not delight in evil but rejoices with the truth. It always protects, always trusts, always hopes, always perseveres. Love never fails.

1 Corinthians 13:4–8

Since love is so vital to people everywhere, how is it that we have such difficulty understanding, living, and interpreting it? The barriers to love are as universal as the need to love and be loved.

I was once entertained by a clown mime who depicted the life of a person from birth through adulthood. At first, the girl clown mime was filled with joy as she experienced the wonders of life. Like the Ashly Montagu film of a toddler exploring his world with energy and wonder, this mime showed a child's freedom, enthusiasm, spontaneity, and exuberance. The pantomime was thrilling to behold as the child freely formed abundant hearts of love which she gave away in total honesty and openness. The sense of freedom, love, and hope grabbed my heart.

As the pantomime continued, the girl clown mime began to sense rejection. Her love was not being accepted. She became stiff, uncertain, insecure. The hearts she had once shared so abundantly and freely were smaller, fewer. The exuberance, confidence, and love were fading. Love was being blocked by masks or barriers.

The first mask was one of hurt, followed by masks of anger, then belligerence. As the child grew older, a mask of rebellion was added. She added promiscuity, alcoholism, drug addiction, materialism, self-pity, and violence, until she could no longer survive under the weight of her burdens.

Her true self, expressed in her ability to give and receive love, had been totally crushed as she took on the negative feedback she frequently heard that strangled her self-esteem. Eventually, it choked her spirit.

The woman clown mime, in her darkness of despair, discovered the source of love—God. In that inner experience, she was saved. She experienced love and felt hope. It became the source of her courage, empowering her to strip away the masks. With resistance and difficulty, one by one, she removed the masks of destruction and the barriers to love. She began loving . . . but there were still masks creating an invisible barrier. Now the only masks left were the masks she really enjoyed. For the mime to love, she had to let go of destructive, limiting masks and habits, even the ones which she liked and admired.

As the mime finished her performance, she exuberantly formed the huge hearts of love, breaking through the invisible wall she had once hidden behind.

What masks do we cling to that ultimately stunt and block our growth, our ability to love, our individual creative energy? Once we let go of these barriers, negative habits, and masks, we can love unconditionally and freely.

Love at Work

Love. We all want it. Why wait till death to ask for it, to acknowledge its importance, and to give it? The individual is the most precious resource in corporate America. When machine tools are properly maintained and remanufactured, they produce quality products. When people are properly cared for, they produce creative and quality ideas, attitudes, and actions. If team members experience deep caring, emotion, and love from leadership and associates, this in turn creates enthusiasm, loyalty, and commitment for industry goals of service excellence and customer caring. People are more likely to be kind, to give, to serve, to be helpful when they have been treated in the same way. Acts of power will never produce acts of love. Acts of love create trust, loyalty, and relationships.

How do we bring love into work? Certainly not by looking deep into someone's eyes and telling them, "I love you." For the moment, let's imagine that love and respect are the same. When I visited the manufacturing facilities of Nakamura-Tome in Kanazawa, Japan, I read a book about Japanese home factories. The concept intrigued me, particularly when I read about embroidery crafts and traditions that were perpetuated by master craftsmen in a home factory in Kanazawa. I contacted the hotel information center, requesting information about a tour.

"Would it be possible," I inquired, "to view the home factory specializing in embroidery?" After a long delay, I was told yes. Since it had taken so long to get a response, I again inquired if it was appropriate to make such a tour. "Yes, yes, yes," I was once again reassured.

Some moments later, a taxi arrived. It took me far out into the countryside of Kanazawa. Excited by finally arriving, I did not question the distance. The cab driver left.

I went up to the home in the country, quite different from those I had observed in cities such as Tokyo and Kanazawa. I was greeted by a warm, friendly, smiling face. "Hello," I said. The woman bowed and responded in Japanese. I realized that she spoke no English.

She led me to a second floor of her home, a bright, clean, simple room filled with women sitting on the floor embroidering over very low tables. I saw magnificent works of art created with gold, silk, linen, and silver threads. The embroidery was so intricate that it appeared to be a majestic tapestry or painting.

I was then greeted by the master craftsman, the man who owned the home, knew the craft, and ran the home business. He spoke no English. Everyone smiled at me. There was still no English from them—and no Japanese from me. I wondered how we would communicate.

Then I heard the doorbell ring and footsteps on the stairs. In English, a Japanese man introduced himself to me. He explained that he was brought in as an interpreter from the local university in Kanazawa. How amazing and gracious of them, I thought, to bring an interpreter just for me, one single person, one American! I felt very respected, very special, very valuable.

Through the interpreter I inquired about the craft. Then I requested something that I later learned was totally outrageous. I wondered if I could have a wall hanging embroidered of these magnificent gold, silk, silver, and linen threads. I heard, "Yes, yes, yes." Arrangements were made for its delivery. When I left, I felt like the most significant person in the world. I couldn't wait to return home and hang this masterpiece in my living room.

I radiated excitement when I returned to the hotel! It was then that I learned the outrageousness of my request. The purpose of the embroidery factory was to embroider the *obis* of ceremonial Japanese kimonos. The wall hanging that they so graciously agreed to make for me broke every Japanese tradition and custom, as the embroidery technique, dating back hundreds of years, was for the exclusive purpose of adorning the cummerbunds for the ceremonial kimonos some Japanese traditions required. The Japanese did so much to treat me with respect, and I did indeed feel respected, valued, *and* loved.

I learned how the "Yes" attitude generates feelings of love. It certainly was many levels above the "It isn't my fault" or "I can't do anything about it" style of service, because it treated me as a valued individual. The respect I experienced from the embroidery factory workers reminds me of the unconditional love I experienced from my sister.

Remember that we all want to be loved. We must love one another, our team members, and our clients. By treating each other as the most important person in the world, as though God has sent us to serve one another, we can have a better world and be a model of service excellence that is admired and duplicated by others. We can bring love into work. This has nothing to do with office romance and everything to do with allowing others to grow mentally, emotionally, and spiritually. As Jack Kahl observed, so many business people err in parking their hearts at the office door in the mistaken belief that different rules should apply to success in business than in other areas of life. The very same passion and energy and imagination that work wonders when put to use in our personal lives will also transform our working lives, if only we'll allow it.

Love in the Past

Please take a moment to think about an experience you had in being respected, cared for, valued, and loved. Allow yourself to relax and bring to mind this past positive. As you recall this caring model, remember where you were, what happened, and how you felt. Allow yourself to fully experience the feelings of love and respect. Picture a time you did something similar for another, giving him or her love and respect; know that what you did brought that person lasting feelings of goodness, respect, love, and worth.

Let those past experiences become your models for caring. Verbally share those experiences with a minimum of three people in the next twenty-four hours, encouraging them to share similar past experiences. Allow those past positives to help you establish new standards and perspectives in love and service. Notice that the memories that you bring to mind will probably be simple kinds of opportunities that we often overlook or deem insignificant.

Pat Cassese, the CEO of Antares Group, can testify to the importance of sharing your caring experience. His organization had grown so large that he seldom had the opportunity to go onto job sites and talk to his employees. But one night when he went to a job location, one of his first employees, overjoyed by seeing him there, gave him a hug and told him how happy they all were to have him there!

Pat had forgotten how important his presence was to his team; yet the underlying and deeper significance only became apparent to him as he shared his caring model with other CEOs. The experience gave him a deeper sense of his personal value, causing him to feel loved by his employees. He discovered a meaningful work relationship that he almost had skipped over, that he now wanted to bring home and share with his wife. CEOs, like everyone else, have the need to be loved, valued, and appreciated.

The Gift of Love

One day not long ago, I received a most precious gift. A person who had attended early Bright Side sessions stopped by to tell me he had purchased a business. He looked happy and confident. Then he told me how I had helped change his life.

He said he couldn't agree with all my principles, yet I was the person he had turned to over one year ago when he was in the midst of destruction, because he knew he could trust me. Knowing his chemical addictions were destroying him, he had placed his life in my hands. He had felt his life was hopeless and out of control.

I had walked with him in this time of genuine pain and loneliness, introduced him to a twelve-step program, and taken him to mass with me. I had been able to openly share what I knew and travel with him on this new path of hope and self-discovery. His visit now was a chance to thank me for this relationship and to celebrate his new beginning. Neither power nor money could ever have purchased this precious gift of love that we both received.

I remember another occasion when a stranger's kindness opened both of us up to sharing gifts of love. Prior to a Bright Side program in Toronto, Canada, I was dashing around, completing preparation for the presentation. On schedule, and with not a minute to spare, I decided to stop in the hotel lobby for a quick coffee. Much to my dismay, I discovered a huge line of people. How I wanted to walk up front, get the coffee, and go! My urgency was clearly recognized by a man right at the front of the line. Without my asking, he offered to let me go first! This world is a wonderful place after all, I thought. (I also wondered if I would have volunteered to do the same.)

Then an idea struck me. Without saying a word, I purchased coffee for that benevolent man. His giving had inspired me into giving a small gift as well. I felt good throughout the day. In fact, I was open for more opportunities to serve others. That cup of coffee cost less than a dollar. The time the man spent allowing me to go first in line was less than a minute. Yet that less-than-a-minute action and less-than-a-dollar gift created a significant ripple effect. I continued doing good for others that entire day. And certainly a number of those people I touched in turn did the same by continuing the spirit of giving. Seek out opportunities to give gifts of less-than-a-minute or less-than-a-dollar.

23

The Gardener

I had lunch many times at a restaurant in Cleveland called The Greenhouse. One afternoon, while lunching there with the school superintendent, I looked up and noticed a strikingly beautiful stained-glass window, apparently from a church. It was the first time I noticed a stained-glass window in the ceiling, even though I had eaten in this restaurant frequently.

As I looked around further, I noticed there were many stained-glass windows throughout the restaurant that I had never seen before. In the one directly overhead, I saw a colored reflection of two men. Who were they, I wondered? The only answer that came to mind was Jesus and his disciple Peter. Without thinking about it much further, I continued my lunch.

That evening, however, I thought again about never having noticed those beautiful windows. I wondered if the two men really were Jesus and Peter. The reason for their special significance to me was that the previous Sunday at church, our reading had been from John 21. In it, Jesus had appeared for the third time to the apostles, who were fishing not far from the shore. From the shore, Jesus gave them instructions on what to do with their net. When they followed his directions, they caught so many fish that they thought perhaps their net would break. It was John who recognized Jesus. Upon hearing that it was the Lord, Peter threw off his clothes, jumped into the water, and swam to shore. When he arrived, the Lord asked him, "Do you truly love me more than these?" Peter said, "You know that I love you." Jesus told him, "Feed my lambs" (see John 21:1–17).

As I began to contemplate that passage, I thought how much it fit with a book I had recently finished reading, the autobiography of Bishop Fulton Sheen. In that book, the only Gospel that was elaborated was the story from John 21.

That evening, believing that the stained-glass window at the restaurant depicted Jesus and Peter, I felt my excitement mount. I saw how these pieces were coming together. I had attended church and heard the reading of John 21 about Jesus and Peter. Then I finished the autobiography of Bishop Fulton Sheen, where that very same Gospel was discussed at length. Last, at lunch in the restaurant, right above my head, was a stained-glass window depicting that same scene. Within a matter of several days, three very closely related ideas and events merged. All I needed to do was confirm that the restaurant's stained-glass window did indeed depict Jesus and Peter.

I phoned the restaurant and spoke to the manager, whom I knew. She confirmed that those two men were indeed Jesus and Peter. She also said that when she was in church that past weekend, the service was based on the same Gospel. That was my solid confirmation: All the pieces were coming together in the same way that colored glass comes together in a magnificent church window.

How often we overlook those circumstances where the pieces come perfectly together and match. In fact, others might laugh at my stained-glass story. Yet this is how we know our prayers are answered—through physical and emotional signs that show us we are following God's plan. God will give us the circumstances and the people we need in order to fulfill his purpose and to fulfill our desires and needs.

As I look back on the experience I had in The Greenhouse, I know it was a picture of the greenhouse that we all live in, this great, wonderful world where we need to be encouraged to garden our creativity. The master gardener of this great, wonderful world is God, and each of us is here to tend it. We each have our own set of tools and talents for gardening.

I wonder what we are doing in the corporate world to feed, nurture, and tend to God's people. What are we doing to help people utilize their potential, tap into their talent, and feel filled with love, joy, and purpose? So often I look at the working environment and I see the opposite happening. People are filled with stress, anxiety, tension, and fear. They have no sense of purpose other than the bottom line and helping a few people greedily put huge sums of money into their pockets.

That is why I think Nancy Vetrone, founder of Original Copy Centers, while she never uses the words "God" or "spirituality," feeds and tends God's garden in the way I believe God intended. Nancy looks for ways to care for people to help them grow—and not only people within her own organization, but others in the larger community.

She's a very powerful example of how a crisis transforms our lives. It is the responsibility of CEOs, myself included, to utilize their lives in a way that produces fruit, not only for themselves but for others. It is gardening the garden that God has given us, the garden that God has begun and still tends. In Nancy Vetrone's case, she used a negative experience in her life to produce a harvest for many others, to give others opportunities for fully living and loving.

Some time ago, I was asked to present a Bright Side series of programs to a group of CEOs. It was a very exciting opportunity for me because it was for presidents and CEOs from the industrial Midwest. It was fun because the day for my first presentation was February 14—Valentine's Day! When I think of Valentine's Day, I think of trust, love, emotion. And of course, the symbol is a heart. This first CEO presentation on Valentine's Day was in a building called Genesis. In my mind, Genesis is creation, God's creative work. Once more it was fitting that I should find myself in such an appropriately named place.

Work is a vital ingredient in the lives of all people. Work gives us a sense of meaning, using our abilities to fulfill our own purpose. What I would like to suggest is that in our work environment we develop more ways for people to use their abilities, to fulfill their purpose so they will have greater joy and belonging, feeling like a precious treasure. That is feeding and nurturing God's garden.

We talk so often in the corporate sense about creating team spirit and encouraging people spiritually. In order for people to develop spiritually, they need to have the freedom and encouragement to listen to and trust their inner sense. We can only have successful teams and successful companies as we allow people to be successful in every area of their lives: the physical, the mental, the emotional, and the spiritual.

24

Prayer

Many of the leaders you have read about in this book use prayer in all of life's aspects. Forest City's Sheila Gallagher-Nadeau was asked to provide the invocation at her company's annual profit-sharing meeting, a meeting of almost two thousand employees. The invocation was this prayer of gratitude:

For many the season of giving has begun. The stores, with all of their decor, reminded us that it was necessary to "turn on" a spirit of giving around Halloween. Somehow the real spirit of these holy days has become somewhat ambiguous.

In both traditions, Hanukkah and Christmas, the reason for celebration and giving came from a spirit of gratitude. Gratitude that something had been given back, gratitude that someone had come to make sense out of the rubble, gratitude that the result of those events would be that our lives would be better. It is fitting that we direct our prayer in our individual traditions with a spirit of gratitude.

We pray in thanksgiving, as we complete another year, for the opportunity to work, to provide for our families and make choices in a free country. To accept the challenges that are offered and present challenges to those we employ.

We pray in thanksgiving for these families that employ us and in gratitude for the portion of their bounty that they share so generously.

We pray in gratitude for each individual receiving a service award this evening, for the years and talent and commitment that has created the character of this company.

We pray for blessings on the people in retirement that join us this evening to celebrate with new and old friends.

We pray in a very special way for those who are much less fortunate than we are.

We pray for a New Year filled with peace, prosperity, and good health mentally, physically, and spiritually.

And finally, we pray for blessings on each one of us and the gifts of food we are about to receive. Amen.

Later that evening, Gallagher-Nadeau was asked who taught her to pray. She replied, "I prayed, and it came to me."

I wondered about my own life of prayer. I recalled a time I had met with my publisher about the promotion of the hardcover edition of my book. Disappointing news had triggered feelings from childhood of not being good enough. A friend had wondered aloud if I had turned over my book to God. Letting go of myself, I had prayed for God's hand in my book's destiny.

In my interview, I questioned Gallagher-Nadeau, "How can people believe this prayer stuff is real?" At that precise moment, a woman came over to our table, excusing herself for interrupting, and said, "I overheard your interview. Please tell me where it will be printed. I heard you talk about God, and I want to read it."

Participants in Bright Side seminars often share their seminar experiences following a program. In seeking to know how the Bright Side experience was meaningful and relevant, I am often struck by the diverse responses I get. As each person is unique, so is the impact of Bright Side. When participants rediscover past positive experiences from childhood, my heart gladdens for the person who immediately blossoms in confidence from that remembrance. Others share the agony of having no childhood memories and the painstakingly hard work to bring to the surface any childhood experience. My heart also rejoices for them. They have begun building their bright side. Others share with me a similar life experience, how they will approach people differently, how they can see more of their potential, how they will take Bright Side principles home or to work.

I am even more struck by their curiosity about my enthusiasm, my energy, my vulnerability in sharing myself and my life experiences. They typically ask me what I do and where that enthusiasm and energy comes from.

No longer boastful of my natural gifts as I was in the machine tool industry, but humbled by how I was destructively basing my life on self-centeredness, I share my magic, my secret—which is really not a secret and certainly not magic: I have faith. I believe in God's amazing grace.

> Amazing grace! How sweet the sound, that saved a wretch like me!
> I once was lost, but now am found, was blind, but now I see.
> 'Twas grace that taught my heart to fear, and grace my fears
> relieved.
> How precious did that grace appear, the hour I first believed.
> Through many dangers, toils and snares, I have already come.
> 'Tis grace has brought me safe thus far, and grace will lead me
> home.
> The Lord has promised good to me, His word my hope secures;
> He will my shield and portion be as long as life endures.
> When we've been there ten thousand years, bright shining as the
> sun,
> We've no less days to sing God's praise than when we'd first
> begun.

I read Scripture, study Scripture, and pray from Scripture. In my darkest moments, I repeat the same short prayers hundreds of times each day. I pray that God will show me the way; that he will give me practical signs of what I am to do; that he closes the doors that are to be closed and opens the doors that are to be opened. I pray that he guides me when I speak.

The most difficult prayer for me is turning everything over to God. Yet I have frequently witnessed in my life the power of that prayer. God's grace, his gift, his love, can do amazing things that I could never do, let alone plan.

My approach to prayer is simple. It involves meditating on the omnipotence of God, thanking him for his specific blessings and gifts, sharing my sins and human weaknesses, turning over to God all things in my life, asking forgiveness, wisdom, and direction and for the practical signs of such, and reading and meditating on a specific verse of Scripture. Those words truly come alive to me!

I haven't always been a woman of faith. My spiritual journey began when God brought me to my knees in 1981, during the collapse of the machine tool industry. In that devastating darkness, I experienced God as my only source of hope. I began to seek God's guidance for my life. Not really knowing how to pray, my prayers were simple. Yet I ultimately found peace, a driving purpose, and an unmistakable passion. My pain wouldn't go to waste—somehow I would share what I learned.

A surprising series of events unfolded as I begged God to show me the way. I was asked to speak at (of all places) a church luncheon when the idea of sharing my experience in a speech had never crossed my mind. Much to my delight, what I shared was enthusiastically received by my audience. In fact, one woman approached me, saying her husband's company could benefit from my ideas. "What a wonderful suggestion," I blurted. Talking to businesses had not crossed my mind, either. Yes, through the simplicity of God's divine orchestration, Bright Side seminars were born!

Often we fail to ask God for help or for our heart's desire. One executive welled with tears as she realized that she hadn't reached for God's direction in planning her career. "Somehow," she shared, "I failed to pray. Perhaps I didn't feel worthy of God's blessings." This reminds me of Philippians 4:6, "Do not be anxious about anything, but in everything, by prayer and petition, with thanksgiving, present your requests to God."

When my former husband and I began to see each other after almost nine years of divorce, my son exclaimed, "I know there is a God. I have been praying that God would show me that he exists." We also had my large extended family praying for reconciliation! My daughter's prayer for a renewed relationship with her father was also answered. The practical sign was the sight of her previously non-church-going father praying in St. Joan of Arc Church, exactly at the same time we made an unplanned stop at the rectory. We later discovered that Maressa's father was praying for wisdom for our family at the same moment she kissed his cheek.

The first time we attended church together, the mass was dedicated to the celebration of marriage and for those divorced. This was another practical sign. Finally, as we sorted through our decision to remarry, a neighbor inquired about the availability of area rental property. It turned out that my house was immediately needed for rental. In the midst of my uncertainty about when we would remarry, this unusual rental opportunity made the date clear. We can never do ourselves what God can do for us.

As we reunite our family, I have learned great lessons about commitment. I also have learned that the media manipulates us by depicting marriage and divorce with principles that lack morality and truth. But mostly I have learned about God and his amazing grace!

An essential ingredient for us is openness to the amazing array of the most precious orchestrations of divine providence. These signs, although vast, are often subtle. To see them requires a more astute level of consciousness, a willingness, in a sense, to view our world more openly. Otherwise, these gifts rush by us totally unnoticed.

How many times do we miss the messages that are intended for us because our eyes are not wide open, because we are not in prayer, because we are not tapped into our spiritual selves? How many messages do we miss because we are out of the current of spirituality?

To me each day is a triumphant day, an awesome day. Each day has very specific messages for us to help us utilize our talent and abilities. And each one of us brings to the whole big tapestry our experiences, our expertise, our knowledge, and our talents. But our color in the tapestry only becomes brilliant and clear when we are listening to the will of God.

God also uses angels as practical signs. Before you begin to think in some supernatural or celestial direction, let me clarify that angels are people like you and me, who surface at a precise time of need. One angel in my life has been my therapist, Jan Ream, of Cleveland. As I wrote this very chapter about prayer, angels, and the hopeful direction of my family, she telephoned. You might not think it a significant event, perhaps, yet there was a profound significance. Jan never calls in the evening; this time she did. She was drawn by one purpose: to support and reinforce the decision Ed and I had made to once again marry. There could not have been a more significant message. This was absolute validation through the synchronicity of events and people.

Right after this phone call, my daughter Maressa rushed to me, excited and breathless. She had uncovered a treasure: a box of family photographs we thought were lost, lovely pictures of Brant and her as toddlers. We smiled and giggled while viewing the photographs. We recalled the love of earlier years, before our family was shattered by divorce. The fear of what might go amiss began to melt. We knew those pictures had surfaced to heal our hearts, to rediscover past love and fuel the hope for our future family.

My life only works because of God. To answer those who ask about my vitality, I believe it's God's hand. We can all have God's hand in everything we do. All we need to do is ask, and believe.

The following is one of my favorite prayers. I learned it from an old Jesuit priest who prayed with my sister, Debby, during the last days of her life.

> May the omnipotence of God, the Father, empower me.
> May the wisdom of God, the Son, enlighten my mind.
> May the love of God, the Holy Spirit, inflame my heart.

Epilogue

As I finish the last pages of my book, I reflect on my forty-six years of living. Long ago, my spirit was crushed and my heart deadened by wounds that go very deep. As a child, I experienced the devastating impact of alcoholism and a splintered family. My marriage ended in pain and humiliation. I crawled out of darkness into further darkness, abusing myself in my attempts to grasp self-respect and dignity. I moved forward slowly, too often sliding back into shame, guilt, and anger.

Finally, I have reached up and grasped freedom. The love of Jesus has emancipated me. Through God's magnificent mercy, I have been cleansed and healed. I forgive my own transgressions, knowing God's bountiful love and forgiveness. I am grateful for his blessings, most significantly for the awesome gift of healing between my former husband Ed and me. I am grateful for my two precious children, Maressa and Brant. I am extraordinarily amazed by God's will for our family. That vision of a faithful, healthy, nurturing family is within reach. Maybe I would never have this gift without the costly life lessons I experienced.

Life is precious. Miracles surround us daily. God reminds us of what is eternal through our suffering and losses. There is great joy and hope in my heart for the future, the same kind of hope and joy my family experienced when we released heart-shaped balloons in celebration of my late sister Debby's birthday. Our mother gathered all the children—Debby's four children, plus their cousins—and gave each child a heart-shaped mylar balloon and markers. The kids drew pictures and wrote tender messages of love to Debby. We marched outside to send these balloons to heaven.

Released, one by one, all eleven balloons followed a spectacular vertical path into the wide open sky. We watched in awe as the twelfth balloon, with no message on it, was released. It rose higher and higher, yet further and further out of the path of this vertical formation. God spoke to us about Debby in a mysterious but clear way that we all understood. That errant twelfth balloon, charting its own idiosyncratic course in the heavens, seemed deeply symbolic to all of us that our beloved Debby was with her Creator. The miracles and grace which we receive each day provide us the physical evidence of our Creator's presence in our lives. As Ralph Waldo Emerson writes, "All I have seen teaches me to trust the Creator for what I have not seen."

Appendix

In building our bright side, we must construct what might be called a positive interpretation machine. The following section suggests some specific methods for doing that. You might want to go through some of these exercises with a learning partner.

Let's begin, however, with a classic poem that describes one person's gradual discovery of the way we inflict wounds upon ourselves.

Autobiography In Five Short Chapters
Portia Nelson

I

I walk, down the street.
There is a deep hole in the sidewalk.
I fall in.
I am lost . . . I am helpless.
It isn't my fault.
It takes forever to find a way out.

II

I walk down the same street.
There is a deep hole in the sidewalk.
I pretend I don't see it.
I fall in again.

I can't believe I am in the same place, but it isn't my fault.
It still takes a long time to get out.

III

I walk down the same street.
There is a deep hole in the sidewalk.
I see it is there.
I still fall in . . . it's a habit.
My eyes are open.
I know where I am.
It is my fault.
I get out immediately.

IV

I walk down the same street.
There is a deep hole in the sidewalk.
I walk around it.

V

I walk down another street.[17]

To begin charting your voyage of rediscovery, I suggest you consider keeping a written journal. It will help you trace your progress in any one of a number of areas. For instance, you might keep a prayer journal, in which you record how and when God answers your prayers. But regardless of your feelings about spirituality and religion, you will probably benefit from keeping a record of what crosses through your mind.

You might also keep a record of your ideas or the images that come to you from listening to and trusting your own quiet inner voice, or intuition. As the chemist Linus Pauling said, "The way to get good ideas is to get lots of ideas and throw the bad ones away." Plunder the world for ideas, and then ask yourself of everything you hear, read, and see: What have I learned, and how might I apply it? Exercise your thinking muscle regularly. Tragically, we spend thousands of hours during our school years learning technical details that may or may not later find application in our lives. We spend too little time learning how to think imaginatively.

Learning to Let Go

In moving from our entrenched resistance toward learning and change, it's important to recognize the various ways in which that resistance is manifested in our everyday actions. The following are some attitudes we might want to change:

Fear	Gossiping
Blaming others, not myself	Talking too much
Withdrawal	Dominating others
Withholding information	Controlling others
Denial	Engaging in toxic humor
Issuing threats	Worrying too much
Procrastinating	Being a perfectionist
Being a know-it-all	Being too busy

On the other hand, there are just as many behaviors through which we can signal our openness to learning and to healthier living. They include:

Listening better	Being unafraid
Participating	Being nonjudgmental
Asking questions	Being more attentive
Increasing energy level	Sharing ideas
Trusting more	Fearing ridicule less
Being uninhibited	Becoming more informal
Being inventive	Taking risks
Being straightforward	Having fun

Answer these questions:

- What did I feel as I looked over these categories?
- Which behaviors from the first list best describe my methods of resistance?

- What specific action steps can I take to let go of hurtful behaviors?
- What small steps can I take today to see some immediate improvement?
- What larger steps might I take to attain longer-lasting benefits?
- How can I anchor these steps in my mind with appropriate mental pictures?

Building Trust

We can improve our relationships by improving the trust on which they're based. Many barriers to trust are the same as the barriers to learning.

Keeping in mind the author Leo Buscaglia's observation that "I am more involved in unlearning than learning; I'm having to unlearn all the garbage that people have laid on me," let's see how we might go about replacing toxic behaviors with behaviors that will encourage trust:

- Instead of trying to control others, we can offer them options. If I feel you are giving me plenty of flexibility, I won't feel constrained.
- Rather than being so certain that mine is the right way or that I have all the answers, I can move to a learning posture, in which I'm listening for the best way and the best answer, regardless of the source.
- Instead of trying to manipulate another, I can try some spontaneity. By being spontaneous, we are flexible, open, and natural in the way we interact with others, thus disarming their defensiveness and adding to their comfort level.
- By moving from judging to understanding, I can signal to others my intent to learn. Through understanding, we move closer to others.
- In shedding my feelings of superiority, I can move toward equality. Trust presupposes feelings of mutual equality.
- Rather than being indifferent, I can have empathy for others, putting myself in the other person's shoes and experiencing what they experience.

Possible Selves/Mental Modeling

The difference between our peak performance and our worst performance is our working self-concept. It is derived from the active list of possible selves which we alone select and thus bring to life.

Our pool of possible selves can come from personal experience or, through mimicking, behaviors or traits we've observed in role models or other images.

The following is a list of possible selves. You might find it instructive to go through the various categories and identify for yourself an instance from your past—your own Red Ball Jets story—in which you lived up to that specific behavior. Then, try to recall a person you might have consciously or even unconsciously modeled your behavior after. Finally, try to isolate your own goal or vision. You might begin by focusing on perhaps ten of these areas.

	Past Experience	Role Model	Desired Future Outcome
Learning Self			
Confident Self			
Persistent Self			
Resilient Self			
Intuitive Self			
Caring Self			
Responsible Self			
Playful Self			
Humorous Self			
Spiritual Self			
Competent Self			
Lovable Self			
Successful Self			
Joyful Self			
Trustworthy Self			
Courageous Self			
Creative Self			

Developing Your Ability to Praise

It's easy to overlook the importance of praise in building team spirit and setting the right environment for success. But praise is essential. Validating people and their accomplishments creates a climate in which people feel good about themselves; they in turn are more willing to stretch to provide clients joy and surprise. As a bonus, through offering praise, we generally experience joy ourselves.

Yet most of us have a tendency to avoid offering praise, finding it awkward. Either we don't know how to offer it (because we never received much ourselves early in life), our competitive instincts keep us from doing it, or we genuinely think we don't see anything to praise.

But we can develop our own style of praise that is neither awkward nor fake. Here are a few ways:

- Make a list of people about whom you can find nothing to praise. Then try to learn praiseworthy things about them.
- Find something to value or respect in everyone with whom you interact.
- Don't reserve your praise only for special occasions. Err on the side of offering too much rather than too little.
- Don't offer blanket praise, but rather try to zero in on specific praiseworthy traits or actions.
- Be genuine. Everyone can recognize false flattery.
- Study the styles of people who are especially good at offering praise. Adapt their styles to your own.

Spurring Your Creativity

Creativity is a muscle. Unless it is regularly exercised, it will wither and die. We exercise those muscles through playful mental, physical, and emotional activity. As D. W. Lawrence said, "In playing and perhaps only in playing the child or the adult is free to be creative."

Creativity feeds on spontaneity. It demands breaking out of routine, even being occasionally outrageous. It call's for injecting humor at the most unexpected moments into the most unexpected places. Here are a few ways in which you might practice humor:

- Give a standing ovation.
- Mail a cartoon to a friend or associate.
- Take a "funny" break.
- Tell a funny story about yourself.
- Walk backwards.
- Find a playground and try the swing, slide, or merry-go-round.
- Bring baby pictures to a meeting.
- Draw pictures of your team members during a meeting. Imagine how they looked and what they were like as kids.
- Read something written for children.
- Develop your own cheer.
- Laugh.

My "To-Do" List

Just as it's important to keep an ongoing record of your thoughts in some form of a journal, you can also keep working toward incremental personal improvement. To help you do that, you might consider preparing a daily to-do list, which will provide some shape to your ongoing goals. Here are some items you might consider for your list:

Today I will "trisk" (trust plus risk) by

_____

Today I will forgive myself by

_____

Today I will forgive others by

_____

Today I will "let go" by

_____

Today I will build trust by

_____

Today I will have fun by

_____

Today I will understand myself better by

_____

Today I will break through fear by

_____

Today I will understand others by

_____

Today I will surprise someone by

_____

Today I will build my bright side by

_____

Finally, lest you ever succumb to thinking the problems are too big and you're too small, meditate for a moment on this brief story:

The Star Thrower
Loren Eiseley

A young man was picking up objects off the beach and tossing them out into the sea. A second man approached him and saw that the objects were starfish.

"Why in the world are you throwing starfish into the water?"

"If the starfish are still on the beach when the tide goes out and the sun rises in the sky, they will die," replied the young man.

"That's ridiculous. There are thousands of miles of beach and millions of starfish. You can't really believe that what you're doing could possibly make a difference!"

The young man picked up another starfish, paused thoughtfully, and remarked as he tossed it out into the waves, "It makes a difference to this one."[18]

I hope this book has made a difference to you.

Notes

1. Carl R. Rogers, *On Becoming a Person* (Boston: Houghton Mifflin Co., 1970), 15–27.

2. David Johnson, *Reaching Out* (New York: Prentice Hall, 1986).

3. Martin Luther King, "Facing the Challenge of a New Age," speech in Montgomery, Alabama, December 19, 1956.

4. Lester Thurow, *Head to Head* (New York: William Morrow and Company, 1992), 113.

5. Sam Walton, *Made in America* (New York: Doubleday, 1992), 161–62.

6. Ibid., 223

7. Ibid., 128.

8. Harry Chapin, "Flowers Are Red," copyright Story Songs Ltd., 1978. Used by permission.

9. Arthur and Ruth Winter, *Build Your Brain Power* (New York: St. Martin's, 1986), 124.

10. Ibid., 125–28.

11. "Jack Is Afraid of Jill," from *Knots* by R. D. Laing. Copyright 1970 by R. D. Laing. Reprinted by permission of Pantheon Books, a division of Random House, Inc.

12. Virginia Satir, *Making Contact* (Millbrae, Calif.: Celestial Arts, 1976).

13. Scott Peck, *The Road Less Traveled* (New York: Simon and Schuster, 1978), 16.

14. Doris Donnelly, *Spiritual Fitness* (San Francisco: Harper San Francisco, 1993).

15. Excerpt from *The Prophet*, by Kahlil Gibran, copyright 1923 by Kahlil Gibran and renewed 1951 by Administrations C.T.A. of Kahlil Gibran and Mary G. Gibran. Reprinted by permission of Alfred C. Knopf, Inc.

16. Sam Walton, *Made in America*, 15.

17. Portia Nelson, "Autobiography in Five Short Chapters," from *There's a Hole in My Sidewalk* (Hillsboro, Oreg: Beyond Words Publishing, 1993), 2–3.

18. Loren Eisley, *The Star Thrower* (New York: Random House, 1978).